SpringerBriefs in Health Care Management and Economics

Series editor

Joseph K. Tan, Burlington, ON, Canada

For further volumes:
http://www.springer.com/series/10293

Alessandro Scaletti

Evaluating Investments in Health Care Systems

Health Technology Assessment

Springer

Alessandro Scaletti
Department of Business Management
University of Naples "Parthenope"
Naples
Italy

ISSN 2193-1704   ISSN 2193-1712   (electronic)
ISBN 978-3-319-02543-8   ISBN 978-3-319-02544-5   (eBook)
DOI 10.1007/978-3-319-02544-5
Springer Cham Heidelberg New York Dordrecht London

Library of Congress Control Number: 2014932977

Printed on acid-free paper

Springer is part of Springer Science+Business Media (www.springer.com)

For Prof. Gennaro Ferrara

Salus populi suprema lex,
from the Laws of the XII tables
Rome 451 a.C.

Alessandro Scaletti

Health Technology Assessment.
Logic and methods of evaluation

Preface

In the current context of international economy crisis, the control of public expenditure appears to be now a *diktat* imposed by finance institutions, to ensure continued economic growth and, at least, maintain the levels of well-being achieved by individual nations.

In these scenarios, the economic evaluation of public and private decisions, if equipped with collective importance, enters fully into the behavioral ethics of the policy makers and technocrats called upon to manage the public sector.

In recent years, several approaches have been developed, in a business management perspective, for the study and innovation of Public Administration (PA).

These frameworks of ideas, apart from some significant conceptual differences, have in common the goal of improving efficiency, effectiveness, economic and equitable decision-making, and operations implemented by the various companies that make up the Public Administration.

The differences mentioned in the approaches refer to the combination of the importance that certain variables undertake in the different analytical frameworks. The variables analyzed in this work are due to the different role of governance assumed by public entities in the network of relationships, which are the central node, and the logic and mechanisms through which these bodies, in accordance with the conditions of efficiency, effectiveness, cost, and equity, protect and control public interest.

With reference to the first variable, a central vision of public administration, understood as a structured body in which allocation decisions of resources among its subjects are made by an organization/institution at the center of the constellation, is opposed to a vision of PA with less rigid boundaries, in which the public and private entities involved align their aims in compliance with public interest through a process of delegation and co-participation decision logic.

With reference to the other variable, in the various PA approaches studied, there is an alternation of logic that for some areas of research, equitable economic protection of public interest is entrusted to the introduction of competitive mechanisms, while for others the same objective is achievable through the strengthening of collaborative logic of those who form the PA.

Starting with the study of international management on the evolution of PA, this work aims to study the evolution of decisional logic that has affected the NHS and the analysis of the approach used in support of decision better known as Health Technology Assessment (HTA).

Therefore, in the first part, this work describes how the different approaches, succeeding one another over time, in the study of public administration, have influenced the evolution of logic and the tools used to support public decision.

This introductory part presents the theoretical framework of reference, on which the sample model used to illustrate how the evolution of management theories has influenced the decision-making processes related to the selection of the different allocative solutions to be applied to the healthcare systems on which it is based.

In the next part, a sample model for the study of public decision in healthcare is proposed: HTA.

However, the theory and the practical evidence in the work undoubtedly show that the assessment tools alone may not be sufficient for the containment of public expenditure, nevertheless, they represent a valid "modus operandi" for a more effective and efficient allocation of resources, poor by definition, among the various possible uses, in function of the current and future needs of the community.

In conclusion, I would especially like to thank Prof. Giorgio Liguori, Professor of Hygiene at my University, for his invaluable support in the study of healthcare technologies and Dr. Patrizia Belfiore, as well as other colleagues of the Territorial Institutions Department with whom the work reported in this document was carried out.

To each and everyone I extend my sincere thanks, it being understood that I take exclusive responsibility for inaccuracies or omissions that may be present in the work.

Alessandro Scaletti

Contents

Contents

Chapter 1
The Evolution of Decisional Logic in the Healthcare System

Abstract In the current context of international economy crisis, the control of public expenditure appears to be now a *diktat* imposed by finance institutions, to ensure continued economic growth and, at least, maintain the levels of well-being achieved by individual nations. In these scenarios, the economic evaluation of public and private decisions, if equipped with collective importance, enters fully into the behavioral ethics of the policy makers and technocrats called upon to manage the public sector. In recent years, several approaches have been developed, in a business management perspective, for the study and innovation of Public Administration (PA). These frameworks of ideas, apart from some significant conceptual differences, have in common the goal of improving efficiency, effectiveness, economic and equitable decision-making and operations implemented by the various companies that make up the Public Administration.

Keywords New public management · Public governance · Public choice · Public administration · Efficiency · Effectiveness

1.1 Introduction

In the current context of crisis of national economies, the control of public expenditure appears to be now a *diktat* imposed by financial institutions to ensure continued economic growth and, at least, maintain the levels of well-being achieved by individual nations.

In these scenarios, the economic evaluation of public and private decision, if equipped with collective importance, enters fully into the behavioral ethics of policy makers and technocrats called upon to manage the public sector. Therefore, the approaches and instruments of economic evaluation do not appear to be simply the tools at the disposal of political choice, but the real object of the latter in an attempt to harmonize and make the relationship between means and purposes more transparent.

A. Scaletti, *Evaluating Investments in Health Care Systems*,
SpringerBriefs in Health Care Management and Economics,
DOI: 10.1007/978-3-319-02544-5_1, © The Author(s) 2014

Undoubtedly, the assessment tools alone cannot be sufficient for the containment of public expenditure, nevertheless they represent a valid "modus operandi" for a more effective and efficient allocation of resources, poor by definition, among the various possible uses, depending on the, actual and future, needs of the community.

The central role of healthcare spending, in the decision of public finance, has always generated a keen interest in economic studies first, and then in managerial ones, on the role that the characteristics of the organization of health services has on the levels of public spending, as well as on the quality of services provided for citizens.

For the social and economic importance assumed, regardless of the national context of reference, the healthcare organization in each country is at the center of a complex network of judgmental value on behalf of its users, politicians and other *stakeholders*[1] and, for that reason, the scientific debate about the study of the possible solutions applicable to improve them, is very intense.

With reference to the Italian context, significant innovations that have affected the public health sector in the last decades are aligned to the processes of reform of PA that have taken place in other national contexts and encouraged by the studies of political economy and public managerialism.

Several authors have shown that, the uncontrolled growth of public spending and the non sustainability of the massive budget deficit, are the major causes,[2] of the pursuit for new institutional, managerial and organizational structure for the public sector (Greer 1994; Zifčák 1994; Walsh 1995) in an attempt to find solutions of *good governance*[3] that pay more attention to efficiency and effectiveness.

The severe criticism that public administrations in Western countries has been subjected to, regarding self-management, unsustainable conditions of inefficiency and lack of orientation to user satisfaction, has led scholars and practitioners to consider the bureaucratic[4] sample model surpassed, unique functioning sample

---

[1] Regarding this, Ferrara (1993, 1994) indicates the need to establish a balance among the interests of public companies, like other sub-balances of corporate management, as its failure to do so over time is likely to alter the overall income balance of the company.

[2] According to Luder (1994), the processes of public administration reform can be explained through the *contingency* sample model. According to this model, the changes are induced by the onset of external factors (reduction of financial resources) and structural factors (political will and ability for top management of the public).

[3] Good governance in the public sector, according to the document prepared by the World Bank in 1992, refers to the logic that should be followed for the proper management of public affairs. These approaches include: the need to equip themselves with systems of budgeting and control systems for the efficient management of human and financial resources, the introduction of standards and tools capable of empowering leadership on the efficiency and effectiveness of their work, the introduction and strengthening of accountability for the recovery of administrative action transparency in order to facilitate stakeholder monitoring.

[4] The bureaucratic logic, inspired by the principles of social structuralism and absolute rationality, aims to achieve the best, starting from the limits of restricted rationality, through the elimination of elements of subjectivity in individual behavior. The bureaucratic sample model

model of Public Administration (PA), in favor of administration models closer to managerial logic.

The public sector reforms initiated in various countries,[5] despite the multiplicity of regulated aspects and national specificities, find a common denominator in research and in the application of logic and management tools, in an attempt to reach higher levels of effectiveness and efficiency.

This process of *managerialization*, or of *"corporatization"* wanting to use the more common, but "less harmonious" term at international level, is reflected in the theories of New Public Management (NPM).[6] This line of study is considered as the general movement which has developed a thesis according to which improvements in public administration are feasible through the use of logical decision-making and private operational tools, when this term refers to the principle and logic typical of industrial capitalist economy, in order to better highlight differentiation in respect to a logic typical of the public economy.

Some authors, including Gruening (1998, 2001), maintain that NPM cannot define itself as a new paradigm[7] but, the synthesis of various independent theory principles already expressed in the past. However, dominant studies have considered NPM a new paradigm, giving it merit for its contribution to the change in logic and PA management tools.

However, in general the author's opinions seem unanimous about the fact that NPM represents a major boost to the change processes of public affairs.[8]

Therefore, NPM establishes the passage from the traditional sample model of PA administration, based on bureaucracy and centralized thorough control, to the

---

(Footnote 4 continued)

theorizes some principles, briefly reported below, to be used in guiding complex organizations: the principle of specialization and division of labor; principle of scientific theory and experimental scientific city; principle of preventive standardization of tasks and duties; principle of impersonality; principle of hierarchy (Borgonovi 2002). Weber maintained (1961), that bureaucracy, although not characteristic of social organization of industrial capitalism and deep-rooted in other types of economies, found its full realization based on the principles of rationality and legality. Rational bureaucratic action ensured standardization and uniformity of State operation. Regardlessly, the universality of law regulated objectives, processes and outcomes.

[5] The examples cited are: the "Gore report" in the United States (a government that works better and costs less), the "Next Step Program" launched in the UK during the Margaret Thatcher government, the various national programs called "Financial Initiatives Management" (UK, Australia), the state reform started in New Zealand and the "Public Service 2000" initiative of Canada.

[6] Please refer to the first study, for a more detailed analysis of the NPM, Meneguzzo (1994), Mascarenhas (1993), and Hood (1991).

[7] A paradigm can be considered as the set of values, beliefs and techniques shared by members of a particular community (Kuhn cited in Massey 1997). The NPM can be considered a new paradigm, having contributed to changes in values, beliefs and techniques with reference to the study of PA.

[8] Pollitt (1990, 1993), similarly see Hood (1991, 1995) who considers NPM an ideological model and promoter of the need to convey the logic developed in the public sector into the field of private law.

management sample model closer to economic logic, as if to underline the lack of differences in economic activity management regardless of the nature of the manager.

In this chapter we will see how the different approaches in studying public administration, which have followed one another over time in managerial studies, have influenced the issues related to public sector allocatives.

The first chapter is, therefore, an introductory chapter in which, the theoretical framework showing the evolutionary path of the Italian healthcare system and, how it is influencing logic related to economic choice implemented by the decision makers operating in such systems, is exposed.

1.2 The Cultural Change of the '90s. Managerialism

Since the eighties, in many Western countries, numerous legislative measures have succeeded one another aimed at encouraging the development, introduction and implementation of economic logic in an attempt to improve the administrative systems and related public deficit.

The reforms in public administration were developed in these scenarios; where the main international experience is reminiscent of the Thatcher government in the UK, considered by many to have been the first laboratory for the development "New Public Management"[9] theories. I respect to which *Dunsire* (1995: 21) described this theory representative of the concept of *"value for money"*, that is, a public administration more observant to the efficient, effective and economic use of resources devoted to it.

New Public Management, as mentioned in the previous paragraph, is the synthetic expression adopted in references to indicate the line of study that has "analyzed", in modern times,[10] the process of PA reform taken place in various national contexts.

Traditional opinion[11] considers that NPM has origins in *public choice*[12] theory and in *management approach/managerialism*,[13] as some theoretical contributions covered by them are replicated in NPM.[14] Of the same opinion, but from a different perspective, it is Kettl (1997) according to whom the managerialist theory is in turn

---

[9] In this respect, please refer to Gruening (1998).

[10] Other reforms have interested PA in a systematic way in the past. It is important to mention the so called classic Public administration of the 20s of the last century, but you could go even further back in time citing the Napoleonic reforms.

[11] For more details, please refer to the thoughts of Aucoin (1990), Dunsire (1995), Schendler (1995), Luder (1996), Schendler and Proeller (2000).

[12] For more details, please refer to Buchanan and Tullock (1962), Arrow (1951, 1963).

[13] Cfr. Luder (1996), Naschold et al. (1995), Reichard (1996), Schendler (1995).

[14] Refer to Enteman (1993) and Pollitt (1990).

influenced by theoretical reflection from *Quantitative/Analytic management*,[15] from *Liberation managemen*[16] and *Market-driven management*.[17]

The NPM brings together the various theories mentioned above,[18] wanting to emphasize the importance of introducing logic and private market inspirational tools into the public sector. Therefore, the new paradigm, embeds the theories of different streams of study analysis, in particular, through previous studies theories of *Quantitative/Analytic management*, NPM calls for the introduction of tools, concepts and policy analysis methodologies macroeconomic matrix, such as, for example, the methods of cost/benefit analysis for decision-making, in order to promote greater rationality in public choice. The *Quantitative/Analytic management* promotes the use of these instruments of analysis because, at least in theory, they should ensure greater rationality in public choice, as these choices would be guided by economic logic.[19]

The theories of *Liberation management*, however, stress the importance of overcoming the obstacles created by bureaucratic ties in management, as they are seen as the basis of PA inefficiency. *Liberation management*, therefore, is based on the assumption that *poor performance* in public sector cannot be attributed to the poor quality of human resources operating in it, but to the rules and bureaucratic rules that limit its maneuvering space and autonomy, as a result, these studies call for decision-makers and public managers to be able to act freely in contexts characterized by increasing complexity, in this respect it is similar to a statement Gore (1993), that public managers are *"good people trapped in bad systems"* and to one by Kettl (1997) *"let managers manage"*.

Finally, but perhaps with a greater importance since they imply a radical change in the concept of for the benefit of the public, there are theories of *Market driven management*.

These fields of study, incorporated in NPM, point out the necessity to introduce free market to improve PA performance. This is because the *Market driven*

---

[15] Traditionally, proponents of this approach have encouraged the application of the decision-making processes of public operators and methods developed from the studies of public policy, including those of cost-benefit analysis. The use of sophisticated techniques in order to reduce the uncertainty is characterized by a matrix rationalistic that the Quantitative/Analytic management shares with the Scientific Management. For more details see: Lynn (1996).

[16] The studies related to Liberation management, which have developed since the early nineties, revolve around the idea that the stiffness and the constraints of traditional bureaucracies, preventing public managers to express their potential, are the cause of generalized dysfunction that exists in public administration. The improvement cannot, therefore, avoid passing through the de-bureaucratization of the processes and the rationalization of organizational structures. To streamline public bureaucracies, proponents of Liberation propose management solutions like decentralization of the functions of budgeting and management of personnel, the simplification of procedures and outsourcing (Light 1997; Osborne and Gaebler 1992).

[17] For further reference on the subject, please refer to Gnecchi (2004).

[18] The systematization of the theoretical foundations that NPM is based on conducted by Gruering (1998) and by Macinati (2004: 104) seem very interesting.

[19] Please refer to Lynn (1996).

management is based on two theories, the first refers to neo-classical economic theory of market efficiency,[20] stressing the importance of competition as a variable capable of improving the PA operating performance, the other theory, instead, refers to the principle of superiority of management sample models adopted in the private sector, as stated by Peters (1996) *"management is management"*, as if to emphasize a principle according to which logic and management tools should not vary when the nature of companies changes.[21]

With reference to the issues of *public choice theory*, which support PA management evolution, from the sample model based on the administrative rules and roles which are based on results and resources,[22] also NPM emphasizes the need to switch from a logic of management notion to one of result, in order to direct PA[23] behavior towards a more economical choice compared to the new scenarios.

However, it must be said that beyond any discussion on the theoretical principles that has inspired it; in practice NPM has taken on different meanings depending on the historical period and the country in which its principles have been applied. In fact, the PA reform processes initiated in various countries, followed by the diffusion of the NPM theories, have taken on specific features according to the particular institutional and political context, even if all refer to NPM.

If it does not appear easy to find a common thread about the way in which process reforms were initiated, it is however, found in the main effects that, the use of NPM philosophy has brought some commonalities to PA, due to:

- *downsizing* of PA;
- the administrative decentralization policy and its process of streamlining administrative procedures;
- the introduction of administrative competition mechanisms;
- the separation of roles amidst policy and management;
- the responsibility for results.

---

[20] The classical theory of economics, that heralds Adam Smith as one of its greatest exponents, assumed that private interest could "guarantee" the fulfillment of the collective interest thanks to the doing of the forces involved in the market: the interaction of demand and supply would generate prices balance capable of satisfying the parties, thereby ensuring natural situations of equilibrium. Hence, the liberal economic policies, inspired by Smith, tend to promote the removal of any restriction to the free unfolding of market forces and to outline a substantially reductive role for the state. However, the liberal position has progressively proved itself not in line with reality.

[21] This statement is in perfect harmony with the statements of the corporate economic doctrine that defines corporate phenomenon as unitary and speculative to eventual classification.

[22] Already by end of the 40s of the last century Simon (1947), diffused a new theoretical approach to PA focused on the predominance of the managerial model based on objectives and means compared to the bureaucratic one based on rules and procedures.

[23] With reference to this last point, namely the reduction of bureaucratic constraints, it is seen above all the theories of Osborne and Gaebler (1992), that, just as it proved in practice, the route taken was that of the processes of deregulation and decentralization of operating systems, such issue will then be discussed in depth in the course of this work.

In an attempt to limit management and coordination costs caused by the great dimension, various countries have "streamlined" PA both in administration and production, through processes of administrative decentralization and privatization or outsourcing (*contracting out*).

The action of privatization of public companies has found acknowledgement and theoretical structure in the aforementioned conviction of the superiority of the privatization sample model for the management of economic facts. The usefulness of the outsourcing of certain activities had already been emphasized by the theory of transaction costs, yet thanks to the diffusion of NPM wide application can also be found in PA.

In the same vein, another common element in the various reform processes at international level is the separation process of the public service functions of purchasing and of supply. Basically, in many countries, following the NPM theories, there has been a marked separation of the person who assumes the task of financing public services from the entity (or entities) that supply them, in addition to this separation is almost always associated, though in different forms, the introduction of forms of managed competition among suppliers of public goods or services.

In the line of power, as a rule there is an administrative devolution and, therefore, the allocation of authority to a more decentralized level, in an attempt to achieve greater levels of control, both in the needs of the community and in the efficiency of local administration.[24]

PA streamlining has been implemented both through the processes of decentralization of services, and through the simplification of procedures.

Deregulation of PA was the result of the need felt in many countries to reduce those regulatory or procedural ties often considered excessive and an obstacle to the management of public matter according to effectiveness and efficiency criteria, as well as the main cause of citizen dissatisfaction of state administration.

At the same time the introduction of the principles of managerialism in PA, there has been, in most reform processes, the separation of the political sphere from administrative one. This separation has been pursued in an attempt to encourage the use of decision-making mainly based on economic logic rather than bureaucratic. The interference of the two roles in relation to a single acting party is, in fact, a source of low transparency and rationality in the choices made by administration, so this separation was called for in an attempt to provide greater *accountability* to PA operations through a better understanding of the behavior and the results obtained by each acting party.[25]

---

[24] It should be noted that the process of decentralization has had different degrees of intensity in different countries depending on the institutional context of reference. For example, Anessi Pessina and Cantù (2001: 70) identify three different ways to implement ways and degrees through which the processes of decentralization, devolution, federalism, vertical subsidiary.

[25] In fact, often, this separation of roles appears only as a formal as evidenced by the numerous news stories reported in our country and abroad.

In line with this, the NPM has favored the introduction of management by objectives in addition to the classical PA logic based on compliance of procedures, rules and the legality of acts. This new approach has often been closely linked to the operating systems amendment of personnel management and, in particular, has approved the introduction of variable remuneration linked to achieving the desired results even in PA.[26]

As part of introducing new operating systems for the development of a PA management based on the empowerment of the results, in addition to those related to personnel, accounting tools clearly coming from the private world cannot be forgotten, such as the budget, the report, and, more generally, the accounting tools which have as their object the study of changes in the components of the economic and financial management of PA, the same will be further discussed in later chapters.

1.3 The Growth of Business Logic in Decision-Making

The first studies on NPM considered its principles universal and as such equally applicable to different contexts of the public sector. However, the NPM results desired were slow in coming, testifying a difficulty in the application of theories.[27]

In particular, the difficulty of measuring utility in monetary terms has created considerable obstacles to the changes in organizations, highlighting the limits in the ambitions of NPM to transfer the logic of the business world[28] to the public sector, in an "almost automatic" and uncritical way.

Therefore, after the first distinguished studies[29] on the limits of new public managerialism, starting from the second half of the 90s, NPM goes through a new phase that of the implementation of its theories.

These studies indicated the need for a focus on the characteristics of the external environment preparatory to the decisions to be taken in PA.[30]

In fact NPM, in professing the superiority of private sector logic, assigned the specific context of PA a secondary role because the belief that change should occur

---

[26] Also in this case, practice has often failed to comply with expectations of the theory, to consider the variable compensation as ancillary component of remuneration is not necessarily linked to the achievement of specific objectives.

[27] "Empirical studies into the factual reality of management are scarcer than the many theories" Kickert (1994a).

[28] See Ashburner (1994) and Meneguzzo (1995).

[29] Kooiman and Van Vliet (1993), Minogue et al. (1998), Kickert (1995a).

[30] Consistent with studies conducted according to the contingency theory model, are the organizational and environmental precondition determine, even in the presence of the same external stimuli to change, significant differences in the results obtained with the processes of change, so any innovation process should be preceded by an analysis of the context in order to avoid a mechanistic introduction of the not in line with new logical.

"spontaneously" through the introduction of market mechanisms was dominant (Rhodes 1997).

Starting from the 90s, from the same pioneer Countries involved in the reform process of PA, emerged a new sample model, the so-called *Public Governance*, and characterized by the re-evaluation of the public sector specific requirements in the recovery process of the conditions of efficiency, effectiveness and economy of PA. It develops a school of thought according to which the logic of strictly economic evaluation is not the only possible method for decisions-making of public importance, taking as example *Decision Analysis*,[31] the latter being a decision logic not purely economic it is based on tools such as interviews or empirical evidence like *learning by doing* through which the decision-maker understands the needs of the community.

Therefore, there is a reassessment of the systemic dimension of public activity and, consequently, scholars continue to highlight the role of PA in the social context, calling for reforms, not only strictly related to recovery of efficiency, but able to offer new logic and specific tools for the governing of the whole system of relationship between the acting parties involved in the processes of change.[32]

In this logic, the process of public administration reform must not only allow the pursuit of efficiency and effectiveness, but it must ensure control, account-ability, transparency and participation,[33] basically, a different school of thought calls for a moderate use of utility measurement, as basis for public decisions, in monetary terms as.

Therefore, *Public Governance* (PG), according to Meneguzzo (1997), although starting from the assumptions of the managerialistic theories, represents an evo-lution, if not an overrun of the same.[34]

Such development gives proof of the aforementioned incremental nature of the NPM paradigm, in particular the PG is inspired by the criticism brought forward by the public operators and by the empirical failures that accused NPM of being too close to the private enterprise world and, therefore, unable to highlight the specific decision-making and management of public administrations.

With the introduction of Public governance logic, we see therefore, the intra-institutional overrunning of the NPM point of view, towards efficiency of

---

[31] The term decision analysis was coined in 1967 by Ronald A. Howard professor at Stanford University.

[32] For a close international examination, please refer to Kickert (1995b).

[33] The activity of public companies is aimed at citizens, not consumers or customers (Minogue et al. 1998). On the one hand, they expect efficient public services and taxation policies to reduce tax the burden, on the other hand, however, ask that their rights be protected, that their voice be heard, that their values and their preferences be respected.

[34] In particular for the analysis of the points of contact between NPM and PG refer to Hogwood (1995).

organization recovery, to achieve a systemic view[35] of the economical conditions of public administration, respecting *"policy effectiveness"*.[36]

The new perspective implies that public decisions are not subject to the logic of cost-effectiveness measured only in monetary terms, but sensitive to the different utility of the stakeholders on who such decisions fall. The result is an incentive for change in administration no longer regarded as closed bodies governed by rules and procedures, but as open systems able to intervene directly on relationships with the environment to satisfy the needs of communities administered.[37]

PG targets the process of change capable of evolving within PA logic of *governance* rather than logic of *Government*. According to Borgonovi (2002), the term g*overnance* is the exercise of formal and/or informal power, with the aim of "creating consensus" around certain choices of change, while the term *government*, referring to PA, is the process of change implemented through the exercise of decision-making power from the institutional system.

Thus, according to the logic of *government* process of change is induced from the top and is conducted focusing on compliance with the laws and administrative deeds, since this logic is associated with a sample model of the public Entity or public company, which has a passive role in respect to the implementation of higher-level decisions.

The key aspects of government logic can be summarized as follows:

- use of formal tools (laws, administrative acts, regulations);
- rigid decision content-, restricted and non negotiated;
- obligation for the parties to respect and implement the decisions, sometimes without perceiving the utility.

With this in mind the principles of NPM are followed and applied not because they are considered necessary for the survival of the system, but because they represent bureaucratic rules, that institutions and persons within the PA system cannot escape from.

In this perspective, the NPM fails not succeeding in making, the transition from the logic of respecting the acts to the one that is based on monitoring results,

---

[35] Therefore, as for companies also PA is studied with a systemic perspective whose characteristics are: the system is open, as it presents continuous interchanges with the outside; dynamic, as it changes over time and space; complex, given that there are many elements and relationships that make it up; finalistic, as it has the ability to achieve a result; probabilistic, because its operation is subject to uncertainties and risks. Systemic studies in business economics reference, please refer to Amaduzzi (1969), Giannessi (1969), Bertini (1990).

[36] While the reforms inspired by the NPM movement focus on a number of necessary measures for the recovery of efficiency, at times so pushed as to seem too farfetched compared to the original mission of the institution, governance aims at effectiveness without humiliating public interests.

[37] "The logic of governance is more consistent with the pattern of organization/institution that emanates economic policies, produces services or regular economic activities of other parties" Borgonovi (2002: 41–42).

easier, actually, in some respects it reinforces the first, not always able to evaluate *outcomes* of decisions, focusing only on the aims of efficiency.

Differently, according to the logic of governance, PA reform process follows a double logic, both *top–down* and *bottom–up*, in order to promote consultation and the consent of undertaken change process. In this logic, no decision maker plays an important role, but there are numerous interactions between a plurality of decision-makers and acting parties. This entails also the evolution of the horizons of decision-making, respectively, from output analysis to *outcome* analysis.

Its characteristics can be summarized as follows for the presence of:

- mainly informal logic implementation, with the aim of creating the conditions for the acknowledgement of instruments and formal paperwork required necessary for change;
- concrete and measurable goals, even in terms of quality and not just monetary to decide and assess the validity of the decisions. In practice it allows the acting parties involved to understand and evaluate the utility of the current processes of change;
- discretionary freedom of the acting parties, who are no longer obliged to do or not to do, but rather to create for them "the convenience to do or not to do" in order to obtain their convinced and substantial consensus on aims set by PA.

Summarizing the words of Borgonovi, the adoption of a governance approach offers "the ability to take into account the diversity of interests in the adoption of policies, guidelines, choices that align interests toward mutually acceptable solutions" in order to overcome the obstacles met on strict application of NPM.

Public Governance, therefore, promoting, the adoption of a *governance* approach, allows the implementation of new modes of governance and coordination of PA in order to overcome the automation linked to market mechanisms set in the first phase of NPM, thus allowing a greater ability to solve the problems of complexity, differentiation and dynamism typical of public environment[38] (Table 1.1).

Moreover, with the theories of Public Governance, the hypothesis of public management seems to have reversed, according to it, the processes of change involving the PA involves the offices first and then the environment external to it.[39] With PG the introduction of management systems is done both through a change in the role of the Country, that first and foremost through the cultural change of public managers, and more generally of all the acting parties involved in the process of *managerialization*.

---

[38] For an in depth analysis on the meaning of the concepts of complexity, differentiation and dynamic public environment, please refer to Kickert (1994b).

[39] According to Kooiman and Van Vliet (1993) the characteristic of PG is to start from the analysis of the external environment in order to define the different policies within PA, namely PG reverses the logic of NPM to assign itself priority to inside measures and only later decide to look at the relationship between public and environment.

Table 1.1 Comparison of synthesis between NPM and public governance

New public management	Public governance
Pursuit of organizational efficiency	Pursuit of results (outcomes) shared with the community
Competition as a means for improving efficiency	Fixing of specific standards and targets to improve effectiveness and appropriateness
Responsibility for the achievement of efficiency	Responsibility for the achievement *outcome*
Development of partnerships if functional to the achievement of efficiency	Development of partnerships as a method of choice for the achievement of *outcomes*
Relations with the public governed through limited feedback tools (complaints, market research)	Relationship with the public through concrete planning of public services

Source Adapted by Mc Laughlin et al. (2002)

With reference to the two processes of change, we are witnessing an evolution of the role of State from absolute control to regulator, while for the offices we are witnessing a shift from the role of executive *public servant* or of a person who acts on the basis of traditional administrative fairness, to the figure of the public manager that is of a the manager responsible for the fulfillment of public interest and achievement of aims to him instrumental.[40]

To the PG paradigm, according to some authors,[41] is given the ability to systemize institutions, both public and private, that participate in the fulfillment of public need, directing them towards a common and shared vision of public interest.[42] From the consideration that governments operate in a context of interdependence compared to other social and economic systems[43] derives also that *governance* is seen as a network action and positive conclusion.[44]

In order to understand the development process that led to the paradigm of Public Governance, it is interesting to analyze the sample model of the *"five Rs"* offered by Jones and Thompson (1997), respectively: restructure, reshape, reinvent, realign and rethink.

The first R—Renovate—means eliminating everything that does not contribute to the value of the service/product supplied to the user. In this phase of

---

[40] In the process of change referred to, the public administrator from passive executor of administrative law becomes active subject in the production of rules. In other words, through the issuing of regulations to define the organizational procedures necessary to implement in the specific company reality where the general requirements laid down by the legislature operate, the director the is the interpreter of the provisions of law.

[41] Savas (2000), Oliver and Ebers (1998).

[42] For a detailed analysis on the meanings given to the term governance in international references see Longo (2005: 16).

[43] Cfr. Rebora and Meneguzzo (1990).

[44] See also Kooiman (2003) according to whom, for every acting agent in the network, the rewards are potentially greater than contributions offered.

management change, the organization must tend to the preservation of quality of service and, therefore, to efficiency recovery.

The second R—Redesign—requires an effort by the new public managers, who, in the presence of already existing problems, must make provision for their own solution which is radical and not momentary through processes analysis of key variables.

The third R—Reinventing—requires the development of new ways of offering the service, therefore, a new strategy. The *public managers* must be a strategic thinker, must be able to change the customer service in order to survive in an increasingly competitive world, in short, must have a comprehensive and strategic approach aimed at market and at competition.

The fourth R—Realign—i.e. harmonization of structure with the strategy adopted in reinvention, in order to achieve the desired aims and motivate management and staff. Therefore, realignment should result in a contingent structure and be in line with emerging market opportunities and with the strategies set out in the previous phase.

Finally, the fifth R—Rethink—emphasizes the importance of speeding up analysis time, to thereby reduce learning time. You have to think creatively, using appropriate techniques to reduce the time of analysis and *feedback*, which can allow the solution of real problems starting from symptoms alone. "Rethinking requires a better and faster evaluation of service performance thanks to the use of market research and other techniques, and a more rapid judgment as to how to improve service and market strategy" (Jones and Thompson 1997).

The construction of a shared vision, a vision that considers objectives outside the company its own, could increase speed and organizational flexibility.

Therefore, the principles on which Public Governance is based can be summarized in[45]:

- orientation to external environment, in particular to economic and social development and to specificities of PA;
- administration and coordination of networks and complex networks in the social system;
- centrality of interaction with acting parties at various levels in the political and social context.

Therefore, development of Public Governance logic, gives impetus to a more flexible public intervention and partnership of acting parties who participate in the PA system in various ways.

For this reason, the concept of governance in the sense of a sample model for the organization and management of economic relations[46] can be applied both

---

[45] Please refer to Meneguzzo (1995: 506).

[46] In accordance with the principles of consent, and the criteria of economic efficiency and functionality and of concrete technical, organizational, economic and social feasibility, i.e. taking into account "diversity of interests to adopt policies, guidelines and choices able to align interests toward mutually acceptable solutions" (Borgonovi 2002: 42).

within PA and external relationships between the PA and the external *stakeholders* (households, businesses and social forces, etc.).[47]

The progressive attention to governance logic in relationships with the community is evident in many of the reform measures adopted in the course of the last few years in various countries.

In Italy, the participation of citizens in decision-making, already covered by L. 142/1990 (as amended and supplemented by Legislative Decree 265/1999) and L. 241/1990, has gradually expanded to provide for and encourage the development of "networks of stakeholders" for the planning and execution of measures.

This process, already taken place in the United Kingdom and the United States, has led to the passing of the competitive sample model of relationship management between PA and *stakeholders* and to the development of the process of "Reinventing Government" (Osborne and Gaebler 1992) which aims at developing new ways of offering public services, without excluding non-competitive relationships between private and public sectors.

The study of public *networks*, as already demonstrated for some time by scholars (Kickert et al. 1997), shows the current trend of the studies of *public management* to the approach of "*Network Management*". In a solution of continuity with the approach of *Public Governance, Network Management* considers the systemic nature and multidimensional activity relevant of entities and public companies, rejecting the existence of only competitive relationship between private and public sectors. Therefore, in the logic of Network Management, the public and private is part of a "network" in which each acting party in pursuing their own particular interests, pursue common interests in a relationship of mutual dependency among all the acting party of the network. Each acting party controls critical resources for the pursuit of the common objective and depends on the other acting party for the resources not in their possession. The operation of the public *network*[48] is delegated to the ability of PA to exercise the *governance* of the system, governing the relationships of the various acting party in order to reconcile the interests and guide their behavior towards the pursuit of the common objective, represented by the satisfaction of a specific public need.

Consequently, in the perspective of network management the solutions to be taken to reform PA aim at developing collective action. Thus, Public Management becomes the "*governance of complex networks in specific social context*" (Kichert et al. 1997).

---

[47] Further on in this work, the relationship between PA and the system of acting party who in various ways are involved in supplying health goods and services will be analyzed.

[48] Regarding public interest networks, see Longo (2005: 34 ff), Kickert (1994b).

References

Amaduzzi A (1969) L'azienda nel suo sistema e nell'ordine delle sue rilevazioni. Utet, Torino

Annessi Pessina E, Cantù E (2001) L'aziendalizzazione della sanità in Italia. Egea, Milano

Arrow KJ (1951) Social choice and individual values. Wiley, New York

Arrow KJ (1963) Social choice and individual values. Wiley, New York

Ashburner A (1994) The composition of NHS trusts board. Health Serv Manage Res 7(3)

Aucoin P (1990) Administrative reform in public management: paradigms, principles, paradoxes and pendulums. Gov Int J Policy Adm 3:115–137

Bertini U (1990) Il sistema d'azienda. Schema di analisi. Giappichelli, Torino

Borgonovi E (1996, 2000, 2002), Principi e sistemi aziendali per le amministrazioni pubbliche. Egea, Milano

Buchanan JM, Tullock G (1962) The calculus of consent: logical foundations of constitutional democracy. Ann Arbor 1962. University of Michigan Press, Michigan

Dunsire A (1995) Administrative theory in the 1980s: a viewpoint. Public Adm 75

Enteman W (1993) Managerialism: the emergence of a new ideology. The University of Wisconson Press, Wisconsin

Ferrara G (1993) Economicità e solidarietà nei servizi sanitari. Atti II Convegno Annuale SVIMAP La programmazione e il controllo nelle aziende sanitarie pubbliche, Cagliari, 1993

Ferrara G (1994) Il rapporto impresa-ambiente: la ricerca nelle disci-pline economico-aziendali, Economia e diritto del terziario 6

Giannessi E (1969) Considerazioni critiche intorno al concetto di azienda. In: AA. VV (eds) Scritti in onore di G. Dell'Amore, Saggi di discipline aziendali e sociali, vol I, Giuffrè, Milano

Gnecchi F (2004) I rapporti tra imprese di pubblici servizi ed enti lo-cali. Symphonya—Emerging Issues in Management, Issue 1, ISTEI-Università Milano-Bicocca

Gore A (1993) From red tape to results. Creating a government that works better and costs less. Government Printing Office, Washington, D.C

Greer P (1994) Transforming central government: the next steps initiative. Buckingham and Open University Press, Philadelphia

Gruening G (1998) Origini e basi teoriche del new public management. Azienda Pubblica 6

Gruening G (2001) Origin and theoretical basis of new public management. Int Public Manage J 4:1–25

Hogwood B (1995) Patterns and diversity in administrative reform. Conferenza del Gruppo Europeo della Pubblica Amministrazione dell'Istituto Internazionale di Scienze Amministrative su Approcci europei ed americani al management pubblico, Amsterdam Settembre 1995

Hood C (1991) Public management for all seasons? Public Adm 69:3–19

Hood C (1995) The new public management in the 1980s: variations on a theme. Acc Organ Soc 20:93–109

Jones LL, Thompson F (1997) L'implementazione strategica del New public management. Azienda Pubblica 6

Kettl DF (1997) The global revolution in public management: driving themes, missing links. J Policy Anal Manage 16:446–462

Kickert WJM (1994a) Administrative reform in British, Dutch and Danish Civil service: towards policy making core departments and autonomous executive agencies. Erasmus University Rotterdam, Rotterdam

Kickert WJM (1994b) Complexity, governance and dynamics: conceptual explorations of public network management. In: Kooiman J (ed) Modern governance. New government-society interactions. Thousand Oaks, New Delhi: Sage, London

Kickert WJM (1995a) Public governance in the Netherlands. An alternative to Anglo American managerialism. In: Conferenza del Gruppo europeo della Pubblica Amministrazione dell'Istituto internazionale di Scienze Amministrative su Approcci europei ed americani al management pubblico. Amsterdam Settembre 1995

Kickert WJM (1995b) Steering at a distance: a new paradigm of public governance in Dutch higher education. Governance 8(1)

Kickert W, Klijn EH, Koppenjan JFM (eds) (1997) Managing complex networks, strategies for the public sector. Sage Publications, London

Kooiman J (2003) Governing as governance. Sage Publication, London

Kooiman J, Van Vliet M (1993) Governance and public management. In: Eljassen KA, Kooiman J (eds) Managing public organizations, lessons from contemporary European experience. Sage Publications, London

Longo F (2005) Governance dei network di pubblico interesse. Egea, Milano

Light PC (1997) The tides of reform: making government work press. Yale University Press, New Haven, CT

Luder K (1994) Accounting for change: market forces and managerialism in the public sector. Speyer arbeitshefte, Speyer

Luder K (1996) Triumph des Marktes im oeffentlichen Sektor?—Eini-ge Anmerkungen zur aktuellen Verwaltungsreformdiskussion. Die o-effentliche Verwaltung 49

Lynn LE (1996) Public management as art, science and profession. Chatman House, New York

Macinati M (2004) Le relazioni interaziendali di collaborazione in sa-nità. FrancoAngeli, Milano

Mascarenhas RC (1993) Building an enterprise culture in the public sector: reform of the public sector in Australia, Britain and New Zealand. Public Adm Rev 4

Massey A (1997) Globalization and marketization of government services. Macmillan, London

Mclaughlin K, Osborne SP, Ferlie E (2002) New public management: current trends and future prospects. Routledge, London

Meneguzzo M (1994) Reiventare la sanità statunitense. Teorie e scelte manageriali. Mecosan 12

Meneguzzo M (1995) Dal New public management alla public governance: il pendolo della ricerca sulla amministrazione pubblica. Azien-da Pubblica 1

Meneguzzo M (1997) Ripensare la modernizzazione amministrativa e il New public management. L'esperienza italiana: innovazione dal basso e sviluppo della governance locale. Azienda Pubblica 6

Minogue M, Polidano C, Hulme D (1998) Beyond the new public management: changing ideas and practices in governance. Wayne Parsons, London

Naschold F, Oppen M, Tondorf K, Wegener A (1995) Neue Staedte braucht das Land—Public Governance: Strukturen, Prozesse und Wir-kungen kommunaler Innovationsstrategien. In Europa—Eine Projekt-skizze, Berlin 1995, Wissenschaftszentrum Berlin

Oliver A, Ebers M (1998) Networking network studies: analysis of conceptual configurations in the study of interorganizational relationships. Organ Stud 19:549–583

Osborne D, Gaebler T (1992) Reiventing Government: how the entrepreneurial spirit is transforming the public sector. Penguin, New York

Peters BG (1996) The future of governing: four emerging models. The University Press of Kansas, Lawrence

Pollitt C (1990) Managerialism and the public services: the anglo American experience. Basil Blackwell, Oxford

Pollitt C (1993) Managerialism and the public services, II edn. Black-well, Oxford

Rebora G, Meneguzzo M (1990) Strategia delle Amministrazioni Pubbliche. UTET, Torino

Reichard C (1996) Die 'New Public Management'-Debatte im internationalen Kontext. In: Reichard C, Wollmann H (eds), Kommunalver-waltung im Modernisierungsschub? Basel u.a., Birkhaeuser

Rhodes RAW (1997) Understanding governance, policy networks, governance, reflexivity and accountability. Open University Press, Buckingham

Savas ES (2000) Privatizations and public-private partnerships. Seven Bridges Press, New York

Schendler K (1995) Zur Vereinbarkeit von wirkungsorientierter Verwaltungsfuehrung und Demokratie. In: Swiss Political Science Review, vol 1

Schendler K, Proeller I (2000) New public management. Paul Haupt, Bern

Simon HA (1947) Administrative behaviour. The Free Press, New York

Walsh K (1995) Public services and market mechanisms. Competition, contracting and the new public management. Macmillan Press, London

Weber M (1961) Economia e società. Edizioni di Comunità, Milano

Zifcak S (1994) The New Managerialism: administrative reform in Whitehall and Canberra. Open University Press, Buckingham

Chapter 2
Logic and Methods of Evaluation in Healthcare

Abstract Starting in first chapter with the study of international management on the evolution of PA the present chapter aims to study the evolution of decisional logic that has affected the NHS the analysis of the approach used in support of decision better known as Health technology assessment (HTA). Therefore, in the first part, this chapter describes how the different approaches, succeeding one another over time, in the study of public administration, have influenced the evolution of logic and the tools used to support public decision. This introductory part presents the theoretical framework of reference, on which the sample model used to illustrate how the evolution of management theories has influenced the decision-making processes related to the selection of the different allocative solutions to be applied to the healthcare systems, on which it is based.

Keywords Economic analysis · Planning · Evaluation · Cost-benefit analysis · Cost-effectiveness analysis · Cost-utility analysis · Cost minimization analysis

2.1 Evaluation Issues in Health

The NHS is a system based on two main elements: Planning[1] and Evaluation.[2] This statement of principle, even though inferable by all the regulations that in the last thirty years have governed the entire NHS system, has actually found greater

---

[1] In a healthcare company, the processes of planning and operational control must, on the one hand, contemplate the elements of predefinition of resources to be used for the pursuit of the assistance objectives that they set out to achieve, and on the other, to foresee activities of verification for the results obtained, in order to correct deviations and reshape the system of benefits and services. In particular, the programme, must conduct a careful examination of the resources it has available in terms, above all, of professional skills and technological resources in order to achieve a fair and proper allocation of such integration, which aims to achieve the predefined objectives according to the daily complexity of assistance and expectations of users. Programming and health organization manual.

[2] The handling of economic evaluation in healthcare specifically aims to influence this level by drawing attention to some of the tools of economic analysis which facilitate substantial improvement in the quality of decisions (Meneguzzo 1995).

A. Scaletti, *Evaluating Investments in Health Care Systems*,
SpringerBriefs in Health Care Management and Economics,
DOI: 10.1007/978-3-319-02544-5_2, © The Author(s) 2014

application in terms of programming rather than evaluation. However, it is clear how the two functions must be closely interrelated, since programme orientation cannot but result from analysis and assessment of the needs and organization of supply. In fact, the evolution of the standards and State-Region agreements in all these years have taken into consideration primarily, if not exclusively, evaluation intended as an analysis of work to ascertain the conditions of economic equilibrium. In other words, so far, a general definition has been privileged that has given supremacy to proce-dural-administrative assessment which foresees a in depth inspection of healthcare management performance and on spending, many: vice versa, little has been regis-tered in terms of treatment, efficiency and performance outcomes of the system, verification of system operation criticality, both nationally and regionally. On the other hand, it should be noted that when processes of measurement testing were activated, it was an experiences characterized by poor circulation of information and little, if any, intensive sharing of tools and methods used. In considering the experi-ences, however, we must recognize that the difficulty to activate the widespread evaluation processes is understandable, since the evaluation function is closely linked to that of inspection, and on this issue there have been major conflicts between the two levels of institutional government of the system: State and Region.

To change this state of affairs, the Health Pact—signed on 28 September 2006—with the logic of promoting a common set course between the government and the regions, with the Regions introducing the concept of "*self-assessment*". The quality of healthcare provided, indicating the need for "*the central level (in both minis-terial and inter-region coordination) not only for the function of inspection but for the regions that require it or at least for those engaged in recovery plans, service and support aimed at self-assessment of the quality of healthcare provided.*"

In the Health Pact, an innovative national role is affirmed for the Regions by way of strong coordination and subsidiary support of reality with great criticality.

Assessment, on the other hand, assumes in this sense techno-scientific conno-tations only in part, a field in which possible conflicts are always solvable, once the mutual regional and inter-technical system of "mistrust has been overcome". In this case, evaluation becomes, the field in which, more than any other, technique and politics meet; an evaluation process detached from the political context does not exist and it is not such if it does not foresee its fulfillment the activation of a decision and, if the assessment is aimed at decision-making, it will be the latter to control the content.

From this point of view, evaluation can also appear awkward, making us wonder if evaluation is really the aim of the system. The answer to this question is not simple: institutional decision-makers carry out their roles mainly as a result of evaluation processes, only that very often these processes are informal in nature and are based on political relations with subjects in need and the professional world.

The limit of this approach has gradually become clear as too high is the risk of favoring those stronger or more represented by the system and does not focus on the real needs of the population and the organization of services. It is precisely for this reason that, from the perspective of an ex-ante evaluation, a very refined new tool is becoming more and more widespread that allows "technicians" to provide "decision makers" with useful information in order to choose the best possible alternatives. There is talk of HTA and specifically, in this chapter, the focus will be on economic evaluation.

2.2 The Role of Economic Analysis in Healthcare Processes

Economic organizations and all of the productive sectors must address three fundamental economic issues: "what to produce", "how to produce", "for whom to produce.[3]" In the healthcare sector, the "what to produce" means to choose among a great amount of services including the healthcare ones, provided by medical and technological evolution, that actually provide benefits for citizens; "how to produce" means to select the most suitable manufacturing process for the production and provision of healthcare services (for example to perform minor surgery in the form of short hospitalization, *day surgery* or outpatient), "for whom to produce" means to decide which citizens have the right to healthcare and how (all free of charge or with a sort of cost-sharing on the basis of per capita income).

In almost all the productive sectors, the three fundamental economic issues mentioned above are solved via the free market through the mechanisms of supply and demand. In healthcare this is not possible, because the healthcare market presents some peculiarities, for example, the consumer or customer does not really know what he needs and this is why a doctor is addressed, who decides the most suitable diagnostic therapy; in healthcare the consumer-customer does not directly bear the cost of its consumption due to the presence of the so-called third-party payer (State or insurance). The alternative free market tool is programming: the State determines what to produce, how to produce it and for who to produce it through a planning process, which makes use of the appropriate means of evaluation, such as the economic valuation techniques. In an ideal world characterized by the limitlessness of resources available in Healthcare, assessment of the effectiveness of healthcare interventions would represent the only decision criterion in making choices relating to prevention, diagnosis and treatment of diseases. However, in reality, the limited economic resources involve the introduction of the "economic rationality" concept in healthcare choices and the definition of criteria that sustains the process of allocation of resources so that they are not used in an inefficient manner.

The assumption of economic rationality lies in the fact that, exactly because they are limited, economic resources have a cost (cost-opportunity)[4] represented by the benefits obtainable with the same resources at the moment they are used in an alternative way. In other words, seen that resources are scarce, the decision to

---

[3] The production of any good or service, including the production of healthcare goods, can only occur through the use, consumption, and the application of certain resources. The resources that allow the production of a good are called inputs: therefore a production process consists in the transformation of resources in product. The production function describes the technically efficient methods to transform inputs into outputs.

[4] The cost of a unit of resource is the benefit that would be derived from its best alternative use.

finance a specific healthcare programme, automatically means, to decide not to fund an alternative programme, and the cost of the choice made is represented by the sacrifice imposed by the discarded best alternative.

Therefore, economic evaluation in healthcare, understood as the set of logical and methodological tools aimed at dealing with the problem, based on the principles of economic rationality, of choosing which alternative resource to use, mainly aims at sustaining healthcare decision making to avoid making choices that are carried out randomly or exclusively on the basis of political or ethical criteria when trying to solve the problem.

2.3 The Main Techniques of Economic Evaluation in Healthcare

Analyzing the healthcare system, economic evaluation[5] turns out to be a mandatory component for a rational approach that conforms, on the one hand the necessity to respond to the growing needs for public assistance and on the other the lack of resource which is needed for the fulfillment of all healthcare necessities. The task of healthcare economy is precisely to sustain the various decisions, in order to provide decision makers with useful information to make targeted choices; a choice cannot be entrusted to randomness, even in the consideration that, once used, resources are no longer available.

> Healthcare economy is the study of the ways in which individuals, organizations and companies accomplish choices regarding the allocation of resources to respond to the public healthcare needs (Drummond 2000).

The healthcare needs have been defined by the reforms introduced over years, giving Regions the responsibility for the management of resources. Consequently, healthcare companies have been equipped with organizational autonomy, especially with the intervention of healthcare experts in assessing activity programmes to be carried out rather than the innovations to be introduced (*devices*, drugs, etc.).

Healthcare experts, in their course of duty, are increasingly called to respond to economic issues, due to the responsibility they have in the use of resources and the achievement of the "healthcare" *mission* (Jefferson et al. 1998).

In the context of healthcare economy a distinction must be made, between healthcare economy, understood as a field of study, and healthcare economy, understood as a method of thinking:

---

[5] There are several definitions of the term "economic evaluation":

- "Essentially, the cost-benefit analysis consists of a comparison of the costs and benefits of a given number of programs that are alternative or competing";
- "The economic evaluation is a comparative analysis of the costs and consequences of alternative strategies of action" (Drummond et al. 2000);
- "The cost-effectiveness analysis is a method aimed at assessing, in a comparative sense, the impact of the allocation of expenditure on various healthcare interventions".

- *Healthcare economy* understood as a field of study involves researchers formulating new ideas and the search for typical structural relationships, which give rise to a set of conceptual tools and systemic analysis.
- *Economy* understood as method of thought, or discipline, is instead a way of approaching issues and non economic human activities, using conceptual tools and analysis to deal with the problems of the sector in a systemic manner.
- *Healthcare economy* understood as an area of study, which takes into account some essential considerations such as the definition of the objectives of healthcare activity, improvement of treatment and management of resources.

With regards to the first two aspects, it should be noted that healthcare economy is a science that, when made available to healthcare experts, tries to optimize the use of resources based on the achievement of healthcare goals as effectively and efficiently as possible.

As for the last aspect, it must be considered that today, the demand for resource is oversized compared to the actual demand, in the sense that the destined user may make a request even when there is no real need. For this reason, attempt should be made to optimize the use of resources through careful management of the same. Healthcare economy is a discipline that deals with the problems related to the effort put into choosing, various alternatives, comparing them and enabling healthcare providers to make conscious decisions.

Using economic methodologies allows you to observe the transparency and complexity of healthcare activity, by relating the use of resources to the achievement of final results (outcome).[6]

The economic perspective focuses on the amount of resources used by a service and the quantifiable consequences. However, it is simplistic to consider that economic evaluations in healthcare only aim at costs because, if so, the maximum efficiency[7] would coincide with doing nothing, which in fact has a cost approximately to zero. Furthermore, to define the economic perspective only in terms of cost minimization means neglecting the most important principle, namely the one according to which the resources absorbed by a performance are no longer available for other uses.

A very important issue in terms of economic evaluation concerning the clarification of all costs (in this particular context, cost indicates the economic burden of

---

[6] Please refer to Innovating innovation. See: Liguori et al. (2009).

[7] There are two different types of efficiency: *allocation efficiency* evaluates various alternative interventions to decide how to distribute resources between various interventions in order to obtain the maximum benefit. *Technical efficiency* evaluates, the best way to achieve a certain goal (Jefferson 1998).

illness) and benefits according to the category "direct/indirect", "tangible/intangible".[8]

Direct costs are those incurred by the healthcare services, the community and directly by the family, to treat a disease; indirect costs mainly consist of production losses[9] that rebound on families, individuals and society; intangible costs, are those caused by pain, suffering and loss of time.

The criteria used for the classification of costs are also used for the classification of benefits, in order to have a common means of assessment that can be used in the course of the evaluation.

Achieving reliable outcomes in economic evaluation is the result of logic and the application of criteria which are not always definable. The margins of discretion, of who carries out the study, are faced with limits in the accuracy placed in the definition of objectives, the choice of recruitment, selection of analytical methods and data.

The detailed analysis of the objectives of the study is undoubtedly the starting point of the analysis. If you do not know the exact objective, it will be difficult to establish a strategy or a process. The description of the objectives should be as detailed as possible, including not only quantitative measures, but also the qualitative ones.

The description of the objectives leads to the identification of healthcare related problems and related interventions to be compared: in this second phase, the main acting parties, organizational relationships and the different scenarios to compare are identified.

---

[8] The costs and benefits are divided into direct, indirect and intangible:

- Direct costs and benefits: are used to indicate the resources saved and consumed by the programme in respect to an alternative choice. They generally refer to the resources in the healthcare sector, but sometimes also include the costs borne by the patient.
- Indirect costs and benefits: in the past this expression indicated the time that the patients consumed at their disposal according to the given health program. In the language of elementary accounting they are referred to as overhead costs
  Intangible costs and benefits: in the past, these terms were used to indicate the consequences the difficulties in measurement and evaluation. However, these words are not costs or resources taken away from other uses, and are not even intangible seen that through the measurement of utility and willingness to pay they can be measured and evaluated.

[9] Productivity losses relate to working time lost caused by disability or premature mortality. Productivity losses are estimated by applying the average incomes by age and sex to the working time lost. Productivity costs for premature mortality consist of labor income expected in the entire working life of an individual, because if the man had not died, he would have continued to be productive until retirement (Tarricone 2004).

The next step is to adopt a point of view and the communication[10] of the same to all the people who will eventually be involved in the analysis. The choice of a point of view orients the analysis and becomes the base on which to build the entire system of evaluation. In this step, the type of analysis and the scope of reference are chosen.

In terms of methodology, the economic evaluation aims at aiding decision-making in the use of resources, both in consideration of possible alternative uses, and in consideration of the scarcity of resources principle. The variables that are taken into consideration are the number of alternatives, the depth and understanding of economic evaluations.

From a methodological point of view, economic evaluations produce results as much appreciable as comprehensive. All methods of economic evaluation are attributable to the same principle: the analysis of one or more healthcare intervention comparing the inputs (resources for the implementation of interventions) with the output (consequences, effects of the intervention).

To evaluate the input and the consequences of each action, all methods of economic evaluation use the same procedure in three stages:

- identification of all the inputs and outputs of each action;
- assessment of both with appropriate units of measurement;
- determination of the economic value of resources and the consequences.

The distinctive feature of an economic analysis is the choice of alternatives, as the lack of limited resources and the consequent inability to produce what is desirable, makes it essential to make choices in all fields according to certain explicit and implicit criteria, trying always to facilitate the choice of allocation of scarce resources. Assigning economic value to the resources and the consequences is, certainly, the most complex aspect of economic evaluation because it attributes an economic value to the outcome of "*healthcare*" it is not a simple process, at least not for the ethical implications.

The term "*economic evaluation*" refers to a comparative analysis, both in terms of cost and consequences, including alternative ways of action. This means that the main functions of an economic evaluation consist in the measuring, identification, development and comparison of the costs and consequences of alternatives considered (Table 2.1).

Comparing the results makes it possible to organize the healthcare programmes based on the ratio between the costs and consequences making choices on the basis

---

[10] In this sense a distinction between information and knowledge is also fundamental, because, knowledge is information that changes something into someone, both becoming cause of action, and making an individual (or organization) capable of different or more effective actions. If the information is constituted only by a set of data entered.

Table 2.1 Classification of economic evaluation

	No		Yes
	Only the consequences are examined	Only the costs are examined	
No	*Partial evaluation*	*Partial evaluation*	*Partial evaluation*
	1A	1B	2
	Description of the results produced	Description of costs	Descriptions of costs/results produced
Yes	*Partial evaluation*	*Partial evaluation*	*Completed economic evaluation* 4
	3A	3B	Cost minimization
	Effectiveness evaluation	Cost analysis	Cost-efficiency analysis
			Cost-utility analysis
			Cost benefit analysis

Source Drummond et al. 1987

of the budget.[11] According to Drummond, one of the fathers of economic evaluations, techniques (of evaluation) can be classified as partial and complete depending on whether two or more alternatives are compared and the consequences of the options considered. The absence of even one of these elements characterizes the partial nature of the analysis.

Are the costs and consequences of each alternative examined? Are two or more alternatives compared?

Quadrant 1: we simply describe the results of a programme or its costs without comparing alternative programmes.

Quadrant 2: even in the absence of alternatives, the description given considers both the costs and the results (in some cases it refers to cost-consequences).

---

[11] The budget is therefore a comprehensive programme in the sense that it tends to consider the company's overall economic and financial equilibrium as the result of a coordinated action of the various components of the organization, in the drafting of which the fundamental elements pre-listed must be taken into account:

The budget therefore has a plurality of purposes, which are not only reduced to the financial aspects. These include instances of:

1. *Programming*: the objectives are decided with the budget, the resources are allocated in a consistent manner, and the achievement of the same is verified.
2. *Guidance and motivation*: guidance, because it provides executives with a document indicating which goals to achieve and by what means; motivation by assigning targets to the CdR
3. *Monitoring and evaluation*: it provides the parameters against which to compare operating results actually obtained.
4. *Coordination and integration*: as it ensures that the goals and decisions of individual CdR do not conflict with each other and are consistent with the overall objectives of the company.
5. *Learning and training:* managers need to take on a more "managerial" approach.

Quadrant 3: different programmes are compared, considering, however, only the costs or the consequences (both aspects are not taken into account). In the event that only the costs of alternative programmes are taken into account, it refers to cost evaluation, if you take into consideration the consequences it refers to evaluation of effectiveness.

Quadrant 4: Assessment is complete because multiple programmes are compared and in each one costs and consequences are identified.

The full economic evaluations are, as has been said, those that compare two or more alternatives by relating the costs and the effects they have on the health of patients. The main ones are:

- cost-benefit analysis (CBA)
- cost-effectiveness analysis (ACE)
- cost-utility analysis (ACU)

The evaluation techniques listed above, are similar in terms of cost estimation, it tends to provide a value of the cost elements expressed in monetary units.

The differences, however, emerge from the evaluation of the effects: in CBA effects are measured in monetary terms i.e. with units same as those used for the costs; in ACE the effectiveness is measured in physical units i.e. in years of life earned; in ACU the effects evaluated may be different.

The summary of analysis that can be inferred from Table 2.2 summarizes as the concepts of:

- **cost minimization analysis (CMA)** is applied to determine which treatment is most economical of a number of options having the same efficacy and similar therapeutic outcomes;
- **cost-benefit analysis (CBA)** is used to calculate the connection between costs and clinical benefits (both expressed in monetary values) is performed in relation to a single treatment or in the comparison of several treatments that have the same therapeutic purposes, but different clinical efficacy;
- **cost-effectiveness analysis (CEA)** is used to calculate the relationship between costs and benefits (the benefit expressed in physical units or clinics) it is carried out in relation to a single treatment or to compare various treatments for the same therapeutic purposes, but with different clinical effectiveness;
- **cost-utility analysis (CUA)** is applied to calculate the ratio between costs and benefits monetizing the cost and expressing the benefit in clinical units that incorporate an estimate of the quality of life of patients (so-called *quality-adjusted life years* or QALYs).

In economic evaluations, the resources consumed in choosing a programme (or technology) must be exploited in order to represent the opportunity cost, i.e. the value that the resources they would have had if they had been used in the best possible alternative, in other words, the value of the benefits which should be given up applying the resources in an alternative programme.

Table 2.2 Techniques of economical evaluation

Type of analysis	Measurement/ evaluation of costs in both alternatives	Identification of effects	Measurement/evaluation of effects
ACE	Monetary units	Only objective-result common to all the alternatives obtained at different level	Units of physical measure (number of years earned, days of illness avoided, etc.)
ACB	Monetary units	One or more effects not necessarily common to both the alternatives and obtained at different level	Monetary units
ACU	Monetary units	One or more effects not necessarily common to both the alternatives and obtained at different level	Days of wellbeing or QALYs
Minimization of cost analysis	Monetary units	Identical in all the relevant aspects	None

Source Drummond et al. 1987

In fact, both the costs and the consequences are distributed in various ways in time and as a consequence will only make sense if they refer to the same period of time: therefore, it takes mathematical methods to update them.

In order to introduce, the techniques of evaluation in detail, it is appropriate and necessary to dwell on some of the concepts already set out in the tables:

- **Monetary type unit** is used in the presence of a target market both for the costs and the benefits to assess. The treatments according to the various tariffs, the cost of nursing care, and the cost of pharmaceuticals are all examples.
- **Indicators expressed in physical terms** are examples of the number of hospital infections, hospital mortality, days of hospitalization, and the values of body temperature.
- **Indicators of health value** are summary indicators of the *outcomes* related to the functional status of the patient, to the satisfaction of the need for care and generally related to the notion of the concept of health.
- **Indicators of utility**, expressed in terms of life years gained valued with the quality of life generated by the interest concerning it (QALYs).

For the purposes of economic evaluation, the evaluation of the organizational criticality issues acquires particular importance because the choice of an alternative can have direct effects on organization and indirect effects on the budget.

The application of a scientific method for the economic evaluation in healthcare articulates from a series of questions:

1. What are the benefits to be obtained?
2. How to quantify them?
3. What are the relative costs of alternatives (which methodology to apply)?
4. What alternatives or combinations of alternatives are the most convenient?
5. Once you have chosen the alternative, which is the best way to apply it (optimize)?

The conceptual references at the base of economic evaluation are multiple and must be taken into complete consideration, not only for the completeness of the analysis, but also to allow the application of the study following different points of view.

The following paragraphs will summarize, the main valuation techniques, emphasizing the limits and potential of each.

2.3.1 Analysis of Cost Minimization

As already mentioned, one of the main problems of public and private healthcare systems is finding and allocating resources. In the coming decades, the phenomenon will be increasingly important for healthcare decision makers given the continued aging of the population, the increase in life expectancy and technological progress.

It can be inferred from what has been written that the basic concept of economic evaluation[12] is "cost opportunity", that is, the benefit we have renounced to in using the available resources in the best alternative. After having analyzed the aspects of technical evaluations, starting from the partial ones and concluding with the complete ones, we must reiterate that economic evaluations have limits, the most important of which are:

- poor methodological quality
- conflicts of interest (efficacy results of new drugs and funding of studies);
- socio-economic differences of the population served, varying the appropriateness of the services.

In the practice of economic evaluation there are still two delicate points to highlight: the choice of the alternative with which to compare and efficacy data under study. The quality of efficacy data that concerns assessments should be

---

[12] Drummond has examined a number of examples where economic evaluations are used to sustain some decisions. In general, however, the use of economic evaluations is still limited in relation to its potential. There is a number of reasons underlying this limited use, including the lack of dissemination of the results, the decision makers' lack of credibility towards their importance, the lack of understanding of the results and the absence of mechanisms for using economic considerations in decision making.

based on a controlled clinical trial or a methodical review.[13] In the event that there are no experiments, it is necessary to refer exclusively to the model that shows the limits highlighted first.

The last issue, not in order of importance, is to decide which costs should be included in economic evaluations. Usually, it takes into account only the direct costs if the point of view is the one adopted by the NHS, and will take account of those costs if the intangible point of view is that of patients and societies. In the case of diseases with a significant amount of indirect costs (migraine, multiple sclerosis...) not to adopt the general point of view of the company (also considering the indirect costs) can lead to very different conclusions in respect to not considering them in the analysis.

In order to assess the sturdiness of the economic evaluation results, a sensitivity analysis[14] must be carried out, a process through which all costs and benefits are varied. It will result in a univariate analysis if it is only one parameter that varies and multivariate if it is more than one parameter to vary. In this last case it will be possible to evaluate the best case (lower costs for a more effective new alternative) and the worst case (greater costs and worse effectiveness).

Regarding the results, economic evaluation when comparing innovative treatment A and old treatment B, may result in the following situations:

Cost minimization analysis (CMA) is among the partial evaluation techniques and is intended as an economic analysis that is applied to determine which treatment is the most economical out of the various options that have the same efficacy and similar therapeutic purposes.

---

[13] Systematic reviews provide a means to efficiently summarize the information on which to base clinical decisions. They have the objective of making the reader aware about the rapid identification on how research is progressing on an intervention, the evaluation of the methods used in primary studies and the extent of the effect of a treatment in different contexts. In order to decide if there is enough evidence on the effectiveness of an intervention or if it is necessary to conduct further studies to evaluate a treatment and what aspects should be considered. Methodical reviews differ from traditional narrative reviews of literature. The later require a great deal of influence in selecting the author to study, critical evaluation of the studies and the synthesis of the results. Methodical reviews vice versa follow standard protocols whose basic elements are the completeness of the research studies, assessment of the quality of the studies to be included and the ability to quantitatively synthesize the results through meta-analysis (Dictionary of the New Healthcare).

[14] These are calculation methods to analyze if changes, in some of the main variables, cause variations in the analysis results in the field of economic analysis or *decision-making*. Suppose, for example, that a system of community assistance is set up to prevent unnecessary hospitalization. It is achievable only if you have home nursing units able to assess the patient's condition and to ensure that the service, which they actually need, is provided for them. However, it is not clear what would have happened to the patient had it not been able to use this type of service. We can therefore try to establish to what extent it is possible to achieved a saving, avoiding unnecessary hospital admissions, changing the parameters related to:

• cost of the patient hospital stay in the event of a admission (cost);
• number of patients hospitalized in the absence of a service (volume).

This analysis identifies which is the most efficient, that is the one that makes best use of available resources, focusing only on the input without comparing the consequences.

CMA assessments are based on the description of the costs and aim to identify the less expensive alternative with reference to the solutions with identical *outcomes* or with less significant differences. The CMA does not merely describe the costs, but verifies the equivalence of the alternative *outcomes*, also in consideration of the scientific evidence reported in studies (Jefferson and De Micheli. Economic interventions of healthcare evaluation. Scientific thinking publisher).

CMA examines the possibility of reducing costs while keeping the outcomes of the various alternatives stable and stimulating healthcare procedure innovation, healthcare activities and relationship with the environment. The peculiarity of CMA is that of focusing its attention on the monetary costs, comparing the different alternatives that produce similar effects on the patient's need for care.

CMA provides lists of costs and consequences of the different alternatives. The analysis is all the more impressive when the cost items and benefits included are documented with scientific reference and productive characteristics of company activity.

The most significant CMA limit arose from the need to compare the alternatives that produce similar outcomes: it must be considered that over the years the various authors who have dealt with the subject of economic evaluation have never explained what it means, to get the "same effectiveness"[15] or, conversely, the "different effectiveness" especially in light of the uncertainty that surrounds the sample data available to the researcher.

2.3.2 Cost-Benefit Analysis

It is an analysis in which both the input and the consequences of various healthcare interventions are expressed in monetary terms so that they can be directly compared to alternative interventions.[16]

CBA is a full economic evaluation technique in which the assessment of costs is made in monetary terms. This methodology began to take on an important role in

---

[15] Effectiveness in healthcare means more than anything else the success of the medical service and consequently the complete satisfaction and well-being of the patient. It is customary to make a difference between efficacy, that is, the ability to achieve the desired results and effectiveness (concept used in healthcare) the ability to achieve the expected results under real conditions in the given time. "Healthcare: how to act effectively and efficiently." Project Noyag. Edited by Domenico De Felice and Luca De Felice.

[16] William was one of the first to use the term cost-benefit approach in 1974, meaning it as a simple description of the economic approach in the healthcare market, whose main problem is expressed in terms of relationship between resource use and healthcare services production.

the last century in the United States, following the diffused idea that it was necessary to develop social justification for projects funded with public money.[17]

Very often decisions must be made on how to use the economic resources for costly interventions that produce expenses and consequences that affect the entire society.[18] There are situations where healthcare interventions are in competition with alternative interventions that may or may not have anything to do with healthcare, basically, CBA aims to compare the costs and the social consequences of different interventions or compare them to the alternative of not implementing any intervention. The basic assumption of CBA is in the belief that social welfare can be increased by allocating additional resources to those sectors from which the greatest marginal benefit may derive.

CBA analysis poses a question to whether it is worthwhile to accomplish a given intervention or not. CBA activity is the listing of all the costs and consequences of a particular action which is necessary whenever it comes to goods or services, such as healthcare. However, to transform healthcare consequences into monetary terms is difficult and it is these difficulties that have resulted in CBA losing its popularity.

The CBA indicator is the ratio between the total sum of the benefits and costs attributable to programme-healthcare intervention. The results should show the costs and benefits excluded from the analysis as well as the methodologies used.

CBA does not find wide application in healthcare due to its difficulty to assess, in monetary terms, the benefits and costs associated to the evaluation of a healthcare programme. However, various approaches have been used; particular reference is made to the theory of individual preferences or the social and human capital theory (Jefferson et al. 1997).

The methods for preference assessment can be explicit and implicit. The method of preference expressed assesses the individual's willingness to pay based on consumers decisions: the choices are real and not hypothetical. The contingent valuation approach[19] is to directly ask individuals if they are prepared to pay (willingness to-pay[20]) or to accept (willingness to accept) to get the benefits of a specific healthcare programme which is described in terms of hypothetical scenario.

---

[17] In the case of public projects the issues to be considered are the eligibility of the project (social relevance) and the type of loss (economic sustainability).

[18] The studies on the social costs of disease, measure the economic resources absorbed caused by the existence of a given disease. These studies say "how much do" patients with Alzheimer's disease or multiple sclerosis cost. But what is the meaning of putting, the adjective "social" and the word costs, side by side? It means to measure the cost from the perspective of society.

[19] It characterizes the evaluation of the technical contingency willingness to pay (WTP) and willingness to accept (WTA). The WTP is based on a sample of the general public who are asked how much they would be willing to spend to get a certain benefit or to avoid a certain problem. The WTA, conversely, determines which is the minimum amount that a person would accept to compensate for the loss or reduction of a certain good or service (Drummond et al. 2000).

[20] Authors have suggested that determining the shadow prices for a QALY can be a bridge between ACU and ACB.

Compared to the method of expressed preferences, which focuses on the monetary valuation of health risks, with the contingent evaluation method all three categories analyzed (health, not health and external) can be measured.

The human capital approach is based on the calculation of individual social value based on its present and future ability of earning. Each person is a productive resource for society: diseases obviously reduce this production ability and the value of this reduction corresponds to the loss of individual utility.

The adoption of CBA, from a corporate point of view, means that all those costs that are transferred from one company sector to another are not taken into account.

2.3.3 Cost-Effectiveness Analysis

It is an analysis of full economic evaluation that aims to calculate the value of resources used per unit of output, making a comparison between costs (expressive of the use of resources) and effectiveness (expressive of result dimension).

CEA[21] foresees the possibility to assess the cost per unit of effectiveness for each alternative; the preferred alternatives, with equal effectiveness, are the ones with the least cost or, with the same cost and those with the maximum flow of efficacy. The logical context in which CEA is used is one in which the decision to intervene on a given problem has already been made and the evaluation study is carried out to identify the most efficient way to achieve a certain goal.

CEA is basically applied in two cases:

1. Allocate a budget by choosing a number of alternative programmes, with the objective of maximizing the benefits expressed in units of effectiveness;
2. Achieve a level of objective efficiency, by sustaining the lowest cost.

CEA evaluates technical efficiency in the sense that for each intervention the cost of natural result per unit is evaluated so you can choose the alternative that, for the same total cost, allows the maximization the effectiveness of the choice.

In order to apply CEA correctly, data available in reference literature, opinion of experts and the prospective studies must be referred to.[22]

The alternatives that characterize a CEA analysis can be represented by a tree of decision that not only describes the choices, but also the effects and the costs of individual alternatives.

---

[21] Reference literature is full of examples of cost-effectiveness analysis, e.g. there is an example of cost-effectiveness estimation analysis to compare activities that do not directly produce effects on healthcare, but pursue other clinical purposes that can clearly be associated with improvements in patient health. It is interesting the comparison of different types to diagnose venous thrombosis in terms of cost per case diagnosed. Along the same lines, two treatment programmes for hypertension are also compared, one at the place of work, the other at the general practitioner's clinic, in terms of cost to decrease the mm of Hg dialostic pressure in the blood.

[22] The main source of efficacy data is available in medical literature. The use of this data poses two problems: quality and relevance.

The greatest CEA limit is that it does not take into account the costs and the indirect effects of various alternatives, so this analysis cannot be extended to the whole community without having first considered the indirect and intangible costs and effects.

Furthermore, CEA suggests that the results of the different alternatives be modified only in quantitative terms (use of resources, years of survival), but does not take into account that variations could also be qualitative (Jefferson et al. 1998).

2.3.4 Cost-Utility Analysis

CUA is designed to overcome the limits of CEA, to analyze the results of the possible healthcare interventions that refer to the quality in terms of health gained or health problems avoided. The CUA has many resemblances with CEA, but while the latter uses physical units to express the results, the CUA results are expressed in terms of usefulness.

From the healthcare point of view, utility[23] indicates the state of well-being that the individual is able to obtain from the use of a healthcare service.

CUA is used at the moment in which the choice of a particular intervention must be made, not only in function of quantitative, but also that of qualitative (utility assessment). Other cases in which CUA is preferred are those that give importance to the evaluation of the discomfort of an intervention, when its benefits are felt long after, using a common evaluation of qualitative (e.g. Improving cancer patients' quality of life over a longer period compared to its reduction over a shorter period, or the dialysis patients' quality of life compared to kidney transplant).

Finally, CUA is used to compare healthcare programmes with very different effects, so it is necessary to identify the common unit of assessment when comparing.

Very often the terms usefulness, value and preference are used interchangeably, but in actual fact they are not. The preferences[24] contain all the evaluating methods that foresee an assessment of the same through expression of preference of different phases and relative levels of the quality of alternative life.[25] According to the technical ability of detecting preference, utility preference is expressed in conditions of uncertainty or risk (the technique is the *standard gamble*) and value

---

[23] The term utility has been used for some centuries now, is used in various disciplines, and has a number of similar meanings, similar but different.

[24] The preferences assessed can be or ordinary or cardinal. For ordinal preferences you just have to reorder the outcomes according to a certain degree, for the cardinal preferences it is necessary to connect the outcomes to a number that in some way represents the power behind a decision for that outcome in respect to others. See Jefferson et al. (1997).

[25] If a decision maker followed the meaning of the motto divide et impera, as a strategy of his own decisions, he should rely solely on the utility theory given that health almost always involves uncertainty. What's more its decisions would apply to the individual and not for the community.

when the detecting technique is carried out confidently (the technique can be the rating scale or time *trade off*).

A solution to solve the problem of usefulness proposed by economists is the use of *QALY* that expresses years of life in respect to the preferences that individuals associate to a year of life lived in a particular health condition.

The preferences are expressed on continuous scales ranging from zero (death) to one (complete well-being) and, as mentioned, are recorded on the basis of standard methodologies.

Rating scale: this detection method foresees that the interviewee gives the health *outcomes* an order of preference from the most preferred to the least preferred, and shows the output on a scale so that the intervals represent the difference in perceived preferences.

Time trade off[26]: this tool developed by Torrance, contemplates the choice between two alternatives: finding oneself in condition A for a certain period of time equals T; finding oneself in a condition of good health for a given time less than "A" followed by death. The duration varies until a given person becomes indifferent to the two alternatives.

Standard gamble[27]: is the most consistent method of usefulness. In this approach, individuals must choose if to live their lives in the current health status or bet on a risk. The probability of winning the bet is varied until the given person becomes indifferent to the maintaining of his state of health, or accepts the challenge: this point of equilibrium is the utility that the given person attributes to the bet, and so, to his state of health.

Regardless of the methods used these preferences assess the results of healthcare interventions by comparing them to the quality of life.

CUA evaluations that use QALYs[28] can compare the obtainable number from an alternative use of resources, or the costs necessary to achieve a given number of QALYs.

QALY intends to use, the quantitative and the qualitative dimension of life expectancy in a single numerical expression. Economic evaluation of healthcare interventions.

The usefulness, in this particular case, is the value of the probability of being in a state of health to which the individual is indifferent. The value attributed to the state of health is the value (ranging from 0 to 1) that tries to "make amends", that is to say, assess a patient's life expectancy affected by the disease studied to generate QALY reference.

---

[26] In *time trade off* the preference are assessed in relation to each other by means of the model of the temporary alternative.

[27] It is based on the axioms of usefulness theory.

[28] The term appeared for the first time in 1970 and two years later some scholars pointed out that the functional years earned are equivalent to years of additional life assessed for quality. It should be noted that QALYs are not all the same, they vary depending on the assessment method (standardized gamble, time trade-off or index systems).

2.4 Research Perspectives of Economic Evaluations

As already mentioned, one of the main problems of public and private healthcare systems is finding and allocating resources. In the coming decades, this phenomenon will be increasingly important for healthcare decision makers given the continued aging of the population, the increase in life expectancy and technological progress.

It can be inferred from what is written, that the basic concept of economic evaluation[29] is the "opportunity cost", that is, the benefit renounced to when using the available resources in the best alternative use. After an in depth analysis of the aspects of technical evaluations, from the partial ones to the complete ones, we must reiterate that economic evaluations have limits, the main of which are: poor methodological quality; conflicts of interest (results of efficacy of new drugs and study funding); socio-economic differences in the population assisted, varying appropriateness of the services.

In the design of economic evaluation there are still two delicate points to underline: the choice of the alternative with which to compare and efficacy data under study. The quality of the efficacy data concerns the feedback that should be based on a controlled clinical trial or a systematic assessment.[30] In the event that there are no experiments, it is necessary to refer exclusively to the model that includes the limits highlighted before.

The last issue, though not in order of importance, is to decide which costs should be included in economic evaluations. Usually only the direct costs are taken into account if the point of view is the one adopted by the NHS, while the costs called intangible will be taken into account if the point of view is that of patients and company. In the case of diseases with a significant share of indirect costs (migraine, multiple sclerosis...) if the general point of view of the company is not

---

[29] Drummond has examined a number of examples in which economic evaluations are used to sustain some decisions. However, the use of economic evaluations is still limited in relation to its potential. There is a number of underlying reasons for this scant use, among which the lack of dissemination of the results, the lack of credibility and importance of decision makers, the lack of result understanding and the absence of mechanisms for using economic considerations in decision making.

[30] Systematic reviews provide a means to efficiently summarize the information on which to base clinical decisions. They have the objective of making the reader aware about the rapid identification of the state of research on an intervention, the evaluation of the methods used in primary studies and the extent of the effect of a treatment in different contexts. In order to decide if there is enough evidence on the effectiveness of an intervention or if it is necessary to conduct further studies to evaluate a treatment and what aspects should be considered. Systematic reviews differ from traditional reviews. These procedures require the author's influence when selecting the area of study, critical evaluation of the studies and the synthesis of the results. Vice versa, systematic reviews follow standard protocols where the basic elements are the completeness of the research studies, assessment of the quality of the studies to be included and the ability to synthesize the results quantitatively through meta-analysis (Dictionary of the New Health Care).

adopted (also considering the indirect costs) it can lead to very different conclusions in than if they are not considered in the analysis.

In order to assess the robustness of economic evaluation results a sensitivity[31] analysis must be carried out, a process through which all costs and benefits are varied. It will result in a univariate analysis if only one parameter varies and multivariate if more than one parameters vary. In this last case it will be possible to evaluate the best case (lower costs for a more effective new alternative) and the worst case (greater costs and worst effectiveness).

Regarding the results, in a comparative economic evaluation between an innovative treatment A, and an old one B, it may result in the following situations:

- A less effective than B is more expensive and is obviously not taken into consideration
- A more effective than B is less expensive (always will be adopted) DOMINANT
- A less effective than B is less expensive (a little less effective alternative may be chosen if not very expensive)
- A more effective than B but also more expensive. In this case an incremental ratio is carried out that is a cost difference between A and B and an efficacy difference between A and B

Although the futility of certain economic evaluation studies has been demonstrated, Drummond points out that, although there are problems of assessment, there are no real alternatives.

Drummond proposes two things to improve the quality of the work and its transferability into clinical and organizational practice. The first concerns the preferability of economic evaluations based on prospective and naturalistic studies, linked to clinical practice, in which physicians and patients are free to follow their habitual behaviours.

The second proposal made by Drummond regards the main requirement of each cost-effective task, i.e. that the assumptions, models and possible *bias* are well described, transparent and sustained by evidence, the strength of which is open to criticism by any reader.

To this regard, a solution to the problem of quality would be to make all the data available through on line magazines so that readers can analyze and possibly reproduce the results in other contexts. This would make feedback more transparent hence credible.

The analysis of economic evaluation has been developed to provide the public decision-makers with more knowledge in decision allocation. However, even if

---

[31] Suppose, for example, that a system of community assistance is set up to prevent unnecessary hospitalization. It is possible if you have home nursing units able to assess the patient's condition and to ensure that they are provided with the service which they actually need. However, it is not clear what would happen to the patient if this type of service were not possible. Therefore, we can try to determine how savings are achieved avoiding unnecessary hospital admissions, altering the parameters related to: cost of patient's hospitalization in the event of admission (cost), number of patients who have been hospitalized in the absence of service (volume).

there has been an increase in the economic evaluation studies both nationally and internationally, little is known about the actual application of such studies in the field of decision-making and the little information collected is not comforting.

The issue is however of great importance, since the future of economic evaluations is closely connected to the use of these studies in decision-making. In Italy, a study, with the objective of analyzing the perception that decision-makers and the general public have of economic evaluations in healthcare, has been carried out. In 2004, the group Cergas Bocconi conducted a study which showed that 65 % of people surveyed (including General Directors of Hospitals, the Departments of Health and Regional Agencies for Healthcare Services) are aware of the evaluation techniques and 85 % believe that the economic evaluations is an essential tool on which to base a decision.

For the application of economic evaluations, Italian decision makers come up against many difficulties due to the complexity of the analysis process and the multiplicity of assumptions to consider.

When it came to gathering advice about greater use of economic evaluations, it was found that the existence of clear guidelines, the inclusion of a financial analysis of budget and the independent researchers' audit work, are among the more reassuring factors.

The creation of guidelines is needed so that economic evaluations appear trustworthy, but even more incisive could be the adequate training of policy makers.

References

Drummond MF, Stoddart GL, Torrance GW (1987) Methods for the economic evaluation of health care programmes. Oxford University Press, Oxford

Drummond MF, Stoddart GL, Torrance GW (2000) Metodi per la va-lutazione economica dei programmi sanitari. Il Pensiero Scientifico Editore, Roma

Jefferson T, De Micheli V, Mugford M (1997) La valutazione econo-mica degli interventi sanitari. Il Pensiero Scientifico Editore, Roma

Jefferson T, De Micheli V, Mugford M (1998) Analisi costi efficacia. In La valutazione economica degli interventi sanitari. Il Pensiero Scientifico Editore, Roma

Liguori G, Scaletti A, Belfiore P, Vito G (2009) Le valutazioni eco-nomiche in Sanitá. In: Zamparelli B (2009)(eds) Innovare l'innovazione. Health Technology Assessment e Horizon Scanning strumenti di valutazione delle tecnologie emergenti. Loffredo Editore. Napoli

Meneguzzo M (1995) Dal new public management alla public gover-nance: il pendolo della ricerca sulla amministrazione pubblica. Azien-da Pubblica 1

Tarricone R (2004) Valutazioni economiche e management in sanità. McGraw-Hill, Milano

Chapter 3
Health Technology Assessment

Abstract In this chapter, a sample model for the study of public decision in healthcare is proposed: Health technology assessment—HTA. The health care sector is certainly an area in which the development of new scientific knowledge is hectic and technological expansion, especially in recent years, has been profoundly rapid. Technological innovation has taken a strategic role in transforming the economy of industrialized Countries from manufacturing economy into service economy. The pervasiveness and the heterogeneity of this phenomenon obviously covers a wide range of complex activities involving today, more than ever, tangible and intangible resources of public organizations. Clearly, the focus on technological innovation is also present in the health care service sector, as the implementation of new technologies can offer a better level of diagnosis, treatment and of better effectiveness. For this reason, more and more information is requested to sustain decisions on development, adoption, acquisition and the use of new technologies: *Health Technology Assessment* (HTA) serves this purpose.

Keywords Technology · Health care service · Health technology assessment · Economic analysis · Planning · Evaluation

3.1 HTA: Birth and Evolution

The health care sector is certainly an area in which the development of new scientific knowledge is hectic and technological expansion, especially in recent years, has been profoundly rapid.

Technological innovation has taken a strategic role in transforming the economy of industrialized Countries from manufacturing economy into service economy.

The pervasiveness and the heterogeneity of this phenomenon obviously covers a wide range of complex activities involving today, more than ever, tangible and intangible resources of public organizations (Scott and Meyer 1983).

A. Scaletti, *Evaluating Investments in Health Care Systems*,
SpringerBriefs in Health Care Management and Economics,
DOI: 10.1007/978-3-319-02544-5_3, © The Author(s) 2014

Clearly, the focus on technological innovation is also present in the health care service sector, as the implementation of new technologies can offer a better level of diagnosis, treatment and of better effectiveness.[1]

The term "technology"[2] refers to the combination of procedures, materials and equipment necessary to apply scientific knowledge in specific areas of production.

In the specific case of health care technology, the definition that appears to be more responsive to the scientific context, particularly in business studies, is the one proposed by OTA (*Office of Technology Assessment*) according to which "all the tools, equipment, medicine and procedures used in dispensing health services, as well as the organizational and support systems through which health care is provided" fall into same category.

It is a very broad definition, not always sustained by scholars, in fact, in Italy the CIVAB (Biomedical equipment information and evaluation centre. Ministry of Health-Trento), referring to biomedical technology, defines it as: *"products and medical devices that pertain to health care with the exception of medicine; biomedical equipment is a subset of that sector, referring only to the instruments"*.

Therefore the definition given by CIVAB, compared to the one given by OTA excludes drugs, a choice that the Italian and international most authoritative doctrines do not agree to (Goodman 1998; Lamberti 1998). Furthermore, the definition given by OTA[3] includes management and organization systems necessary to dispense health care services, an important specification if the health care service is considered as a service oriented to manage the overall relationship with consumers (Battista 2006). However, it should be stressed, that the advancement of new technologies in the health care field has, unfortunately, been accompanied by an increase in costs, as a consequence of scarce resources in nature (Kissech 1994). For this reason, more and more information is requested to sustain decisions on development, adoption, acquisition and the use of new technologies: *Health Technology Assessment* (HTA) serves this purpose.

---

[1] Effectiveness in health care means more than anything else the success of the medical service and consequently complete satisfaction and well-being of the patient. It is customary to make a difference between efficacy, that is, the ability to achieve the desired results and effectiveness (concept used in healthcare) the ability to achieve the expected results under real conditions in the given time.

[2] Some studies have summarized the existing taxonomies of technologies gathered from various areas of discipline, such as economy and management, sociology, and highlighting the different perspectives. They conclude that for economists technology is primarily knowledge and information. For sociologists it is synonymous of innovation and new ideas while anthropologists it is a cultural artifact that people use to interact with their environment. For scholars of management technology is often referred to as "the firm-specific information Concerning the characteristics and performance properties of the production process and the product design".

[3] "Health technology includes all tools, equipment, drugs and medical procedures used in the provision of health services as well as the organizational and support systems through which healthcare is provided" OTA, U.S. Congress in 1978.

HTA takes two different alternatives into account and as well as their implications at economic, social, political, legal and ethical levels (Coates and Jarrat 1992).[4]

Therefore, assessment[5] requires, an interdisciplinary approach with in-depth analysis of safety, cost, benefit, effectiveness, also comprising critical evaluation and actual proof of quality of life improvement.

Health Technology Assessment (HTA) is based on the evaluation of the most relevant knowledge available on a given issue. It is a process that takes advantage of and adopts both the techniques of research, that are strictly scientific, and the managerial administrative ones, focused on *decision-making* analysis, creating a bridge between the scientific model (science paradigm) oriented on performance analysis technology and decision-making activities (policy paradigm) aimed at evaluating the effective and efficient use of resources.

What distinguishes the evaluation of health care technologies from other areas of research in this field is its orientation towards the formulation of health care policies.[6] While researchers in other health sectors focus on the expansion of knowledge, those that deal with "*assessment*" are concerned with producing information that can direct decision-makers toward health care policy choices that comply with the optimal allocation of resources. It is not always easy to complete this task as on the one hand there are the 'sheer' researchers who demand methodological rigor and on the other hand there are the politicians who pursue the aim of converting research into practice.[7]

This is the reason why, over the years, the decision makers and patient's need to have a tool that would embrace everyone's requirements has been increasingly felt: thus the birth of HTA.

In 1972, the first assessment of technologies decree (Public Law 92-484), was issued in the USA, with which, the Office of Technology Assessment was

---

[4] Over the years, several have been, the definitions of Health Technology Assessment: "We shall use the term assessment of medical technology to denote any process of examining and reporting properties of medical technology used in healthcare: such as safety, efficacy, feasibility, and indications for use, cost and cost-effectiveness, as well as, economic, ethical and consequences, whether intended or unintended; "Health technology assessment (…) is a structured analysis of health technology, a set of related technologies, technology or a related issue that is performed for the purpose of providing input to policy decision" (U.S. Congress, Office of Technology Assessment 1994); "Health technology assessment is the evaluation of medical technologies including procedures, equipment and drug Assessment requires an interdisciplinary approach which encompasses analyses of safety, costs, effectiveness, efficacy, ethics, and quality of life measures" (Canadian Coordinating Office for Health Technology Assessment 1994).

[5] Please note the meaning of assessment in this work "the assignment of a value to a service implemented in a systemic way by collecting valid and reliable information on it and making comparisons in order to make more pondered decisions or to understand the basic mechanisms or general principles", it is evident that HTA cannot but be based on a comparison of various options.

[6] Health technology assessment tries to bring together scientific evidence and decision-making by showing the analogies in evidence based on heath care and evidence based on policy making.

[7] It is real translational research that consists in translating research theory into clinical practice.

established (OTA), to develop and disseminate HTA Technology Assessment and demonstrate its usefulness to the political representatives.

With regard to the development and dissemination of HTA in Europe and in Italy, it can be said that the importance of *assessment* in Europe started to be understood about a decade later in respect to the USA, when the WHO (World Health Organization), within the program "*Health for Hall*", suggested that European states identify a formal mechanism for a efficient *assessment* of the use of medical technologies to determine their effectiveness, efficiency, safety and acceptability. In a first phase, the response by governments was to introduce policies to control the spread of technologies with the logic of cost containment. This phase did not produce significant results in terms of technology management, but allowed the introduction of economic assessment methods and in particular the concept of cost-effectiveness in health care. In particular, Archie Cochrane stated that selecting a technology based on effectiveness (ability to benefit from the patients), is also a way of allocating resource efficiently (Cochrane 1972). In that period the Cochrane Collaboration was born with the aim of systematically recording and updating a database of experimental clinical studies (*trial*) and systematic reviews based on them, in support of empirical evidence of the effectiveness of current or new technologies. The Cochrane Collaboration was a great boost for the birth and development of another activity: *Evidence-Based* Medicine, whose goal was to find a connection between empirical evidence and current clinical practice in order to improve the quality and effectiveness of health care treatment at individual patient level (Sackett 1996).

Between the 80s and 90s a number of HTA agencies arose and (perhaps it would be best to explain first what HTA agencies are, when they were established and what they do), in 1993, in the USA the need was felt to bring all these agencies into one network, called *International network of agencies for Health Technology Assessment* (Inhta).[8] It now has 40 branches in more than 20 countries around the world, aimed at coordinating international HTA activity and sustaining its members with common methods of evaluation.

In our country, the main concepts of HTA were cast for the first time, within the Italian Network of *Health Technology Assessment*[9] born in 2003 as a research project entitled "Promotion of a network for the dissemination of *Health Technology Assessment* for the management of information technology within health care organizations". The project was arose from the need to bring together the Italian NHS companies with HTA experience, in order to promote a sample model for technology assessment to sustain managerial decisions, thus favouring the extension of HTA knowledge.

---

[8] INAHTA is an international network, founded in 1993, with the aim of coordinating international HTA activities and sustain members with common methods of evaluation.

[9] As part of the network it is interesting to highlight the work conducted by ASSR that led to the gathering of information on HTA experience in Italian regions.

On the basis of this experience, in 2006, the Autonomous Province of Trento promoted a series of *workshops* and began to explore the different perspectives of HTA: perspectives that were included in the Charter of Trent.[10]

The modern public health care approach in the evaluation of health care technologies should be conceptually seen in the overall functioning pattern of the system and structure they are part of. With this model the health care systems receive input, which determine output used in the formulation of *products* in order to obtain *outcomes*.[11]

Experts should be "challenged" to define intermediate products (*outputs* and *products*) able to significantly influence the natural process of diseases treated, with appropriate resources and characterized by great professional responsibility.

The importance of HTA is also highlighted by the National Health Plan 2006-2008,[12] which says: "...*it is necessary to recognize that HTA is a priority also in Italy, and it is necessary to encourage and promote the of use of HTA tools, by pooling knowledge on the subject, already partially present in some regions and companies*...".

The possibility that HTA process will further institutionalize itself in a model comparable to those in other Countries is reinforced by the fact that the Minister of Welfare, Sacconi, mentions HTA in his "Green Paper on the future of the social model".

The book acknowledges that "the process of *Health Technology Assessment* allows rational and economic programming when distributing equipment, according to appropriate catchment areas, avoiding waste of human and material resources and to induce new questions."

It is expected that this approach will find explicitness and implementation in the coming legislative measures, as the progressive assumption of political,

---

[10] The Trento Charter articulates the principles of health technology assessment highlighting: who does what, where, when, why and how. The evaluation of health technologies should involve all the parties interested in health care (who) must take care of all elements that resort to health care assistance (what) and all levels of health systems and structure management that are part of it (where) must be an ongoing activity, carried out prior to the introduction of technologies and persisting through its cycle (when), it is a necessity and an opportunity for the integrated governance of health care systems and structures that they are part of (why) it is a multi-disciplinary process that should be conducted in a consistent manner with other welfare and technical-administrative processes of health systems and structures that they are part of (How).

[11] An example of such intermediate processes could be as follows: laboratory or radiology services use resources (diagnostic technologies) and produce output (analytical determinations and reports). The clinician takes charge of the patient, in turn, produces diagnoses and therapies, i.e. products for which generally use output produced from other components of the system (lab technicians, radiologists, other specialists).

[12] Awareness, is now widespread also in many European countries, that we need to make systemic evaluation of health technologies in respect to the main elements that characterize its use, namely technology itself, patients, the organization and economic impact and it is necessary that even in Italy it is recognized that HTA is a priority and it is necessary to encourage the use of HTA tools, pooling knowledge on the subject, already partially present in some regional and companies.

administrative, organizational and financial responsibility of the regions will make, the development of evaluation activities of health care technology at this NHS[13] level possible, and in many ways inevitable.

3.2   Current Situation and Prospects for Development

Most HTA agencies were born between the 80s and 90s, and consist of technical structures, financed through public resources, that issue government authority.

The first national HTA agency was founded in Sweden in 1987 with the Swedish HTA Council (SBU) [14] followed by Denmark in 1997 establishing the *"Danish Institute for Health Technology Assessment"* (DIHTA). The aim of this organization is the promotion and dissemination of HTA information, also common a goal of another Danish structure, the Danish Institute for Health Services Research (DSI).[15] The DSI is an independent organization, with the aim of providing support for organizational and managerial issues sustained by the health authorities: today DSI, with a multi-disciplinary staff carries out clinical and health care economy studies, both on specific issues and on aspects of methodology. Other than Sweden and Denmark, also Holland, France and Spain are considered

---

[13]   As is known, the NHS includes, besides the Ministry of Health, supported by the Governing Health Board and the Italian pharmaceutical agency, agencies and national authorities such as the National Institute of Health, the Institute for Prevention and Safety at work, the Agency for regional Health Services and the Institutes of hospitalization and treatment of scientific characteristics, experimental institutes centre for infectious diseases in animals and related entities and territorial authorities such as Regions and autonomous provinces and of course hospitals.

[14]   The main tasks of S.B.U. are:

- promotion of the rational use of health care resources, through the evaluation of clinical, economic, social and ethic issues related to the use of new and well established technologies, and the subsequent dissemination of data collected;
- documentation of how such information is used and what effects they have on the results produced by the health system;
- monitoring the activities of national and international research in the HTA field.

The data collected by S.B.U. are distributed on a large scale to interest groups, in particular to this effect from 1996 an organized project called *"Ambassador Program,"* which forecasts that some "ambassadors", mostly physicians, visit their colleagues through meetings and seminars presenting and discussing the results of studies conducted by the SBU with them. Health technology assessment and Comparative effectiveness in Sweden (Value in health. Volume 13. Supplement I 2012 S6-S7).

[15]   Since its inception in 1975, the D.S.I. has been involved in the development of the Danish Health System, collaborating with the central and regional authorities, and within international research programs.

to be the cradle of HTA. In the Netherlands in particular, the processes of planning and remuneration of activities takes place on the basis of HTA activities in both the public and private sectors.

In fact, in 1988, the Ministry of Health, the Ministry of Education and Science and the CVZ agreed on the setting up of a National Fund for Medical Research (*Fonds Ontwikkelin-gsgeneeskunde*), with a budget of around 16 million Euros. This fund covers technology assessment activities (both new and already established) and the analysis of the main health care policy issues. The projects are funded for a period of 3 years, after which a final *report* must be submitted.

In 1998, on request by the Ministry of Health, a national "hub" for the coordination of HTA activities in the Netherlands was created, which over the years has become, the national program for *technology assessment*. In fact, in the Netherlands[16] historically there has been an institution that has always worked in health technology assessment. This institution is the GR (Gezondheidsraad, a kind of "Health Board"). The GR, founded as early as 1902, is institutional body of government information regarding health care and environmental protection.

In France, the first major HTA project came in 1989 when, a national agency was set up with a project to promote the evaluation of medical technologies. In the same year, ANDEM, an independent association, commissioned to conduct HTA programs, was established by law, with an impact on public health care that did not involve drugs. Its (ANDEM) ultimate goal was to provide the various institutional partners with scientific evidence regarding the safety, efficacy and cost effectiveness of technology, providing diffusion and the financial aid of such technologies in the health care system. This activity involved the preventive, diagnostic and therapeutic aspects.

The greatest propagation of HTA however, came in 1996 after the health care system reform, when it was decided to replace the ANDEM with ANAES ("Agence Nationale d'Accreditation et d'Evaluation en Santé"), in which the fundamental innovation is represented by the agency's involvement in the process of hospital accreditation.

Therefore, ANAES is now personally involved in all decision-making: health structure accreditation, processing of refund fees for outpatient services, and the planning of investments in technology.[17]

In Holland, France and also Spain[18] there is a similar intense activity of HTA, originated in 1984 with the creation of an "*Advisory Board*" in Catalonia, whose

---

[16] The process of programming and remuneration in the healthcare field are carried out on the basis of HTA, both as regards to the public sector and as regards to the private health insurance sector.

[17] Other parties have now proposed and equipped themselves for the realization of economic evaluations in health care, such as:

I.N.S.E.R.M. ("Institute National de la Santé et la Recherche Médicale"), National Institute specializing in biomedical research and public health;

• C.E.D.I.T. ("Comité d'Evaluation et de Diffusion des Innovations Technologiques") in the Hospital of Paris, established in 1982 initially assistant to the management team for investment

goal was to provide information about the use of sophisticated health care technologies. The need to consider also economic, social and ethical aspects leads to the establishment, within the Catalan Department of Health, of COHTA (Catalan Office for HTA), which then becomes CAHTA (Catalan Agency for HTA) that was born in 1991. The technologies to be analyzed are usually identified by CAHTA according to the priorities set out by the Catalonia Health Plan, however it is also a partially independent agency therefore, it can extend its services to private or international entities too, and carrying out commission based investigations. Since 1999, the CAHTA has the role of health care research promoter in Catalonia, with the use of new strategies, geared to the population's need for care and to acquiring in depth knowledge of the health care system itself.

Another European country with growing HTA interest is Germany.[19] The first institution to have explicitly dealt with *technology assessment* was TAB (*Technology Assessment Bureau*): established in 1990 with the aim of providing parliament with, on demand, data and information, to date it has dealt, almost exclusively, with civil activities (bridges, dams, landfills) and their environmental impact. The idea of using HTA also in health care, as a tool for the implementation of health care policies, arose in the mid-90s, with a research programme, funded by BMG, designed to assess the possible use of HTA Germany. Following the results of this project, HTA concepts have been integrated into the health care Law Programme, as a basic tool for health care policy guidelines and for quality assurance in the German health care system. The center, involved in this project from the beginning, and which today proposes itself as HTA reference point in Germany is DIMDI (Deutsche Institut für Medizinische Dokumentation und In-formation). Founded in 1969, it is a body of BMG, which is responsible for implementing and managing an information system of health care-economic evaluations on medical records and technologies.

(Footnote 17 continued)
evaluation in new and expensive technology, it has gradually expanded its activities, becoming the another French (with ANAES) NAHTA member;

- S.O.F.E.S.T.E.C. ("Société Française pour l'Evaluation des Soins des Technologies at MEDICALES"), that is the French scientific HTA society, created in 1986, which brings together experts in the field, with the aim of disseminating evaluation methods and results in France and abroad;
- A.F.S.S.A.P.S. ("Agence Française des Securite Sanitaire des Produits de Santé"), is the agency that is in charge of pharmacovigilance and medical devices market surveillance and has set up an internal commission of products and services assessment (CEPP, "Commission d'évaluation des Produits et prestations"). This committee has the task of supplying C.E.P.S. ("Comité Economique des Produits de Santé")—the body responsible for setting refund fees (ex-T.I.P.S. (Tarif Interministériel des Prestations Sanitaires) today L.P.P. (Liste des Produits et Prestations rem-boursables.) after a reform of the system taken place in 2000) of certain categories of medical devices—a constant update concerning products on the market.

[18] HTA is a tool widely used to start right from the autonomous regional authorities that have developed their own agencies. There is the issue of coordination of activities at national level, an issue recently resolved through the establishment of a scientific committee.

[19] Health Technology Assessment: a prospective from Germany. Value in health. Volume 12. Supplement 2, 2009 S20_SS22.

Such a system collects scientifically validated material making it available to public and private entities, as well as to citizens.

DIMDI is involved in another initiative, funded by BMG, which attempts to stimulate the growth of *decision-making* HTA activities at federal level. This initiative is the creation of the *"German Working Group of Technology Assessment in Health Care"* that has implemented a series of HTA studies on different technologies, in order to establish a national database of economic evaluation, in collaboration with DIMDI.

The group has also the task of checking the possibility of applying the results of studies conducted in Germany. The organization pays substantial attention to the development and application of standardized methods to ensure quality and transparency in its research activities. The selection of themes and priorities is carried out by a scientific committee, which includes the participation of Ministry of Health representatives, as well as other national health care institutions.

Similarly to Germany there has been a boost in HTA interest in recent years also in the UK, thanks to the birth of NICE (*National Institute for Clinical Excellence*), founded in 1999. The main areas of activity of this institution are the implementation of guidelines and evaluation of new health care technologies already in use: drugs, medical devices, diagnostic tests, clinical procedures and aspects concerning health prevention.

At international level, NICE is definitely an innovative experiment, as it is the first national agency capable of producing analysis and guidelines covering the entire spectrum of health care technologies, understood in the broadest sense. Health technologies to be analyzed are selected by the *Department of Health*, the English Department of Health (*Department of Health*, D.H.) and the National Assembly for Wales (National Assembly for Wales, W.A.). These authorities have the task of selecting the technologies to be evaluated by NICE on the basis of four criteria: possible clinical benefits, involvement in specific health care policy programmes, the possible impact on NHS resources (National Health Service), and possible added value produced by NICE guidelines. The HTA National Programme is funded under the NHS Research and Development Programme. It is coordinated by the *National Coordinating Centre for HTA* (NCC HTA), set up in the *Wessex Institute for Health Research and Development* at the University of Southampton.

This program aims to produce and disseminate scientific results concerning quality in the use of health care technologies in terms of cost and effectiveness, through reports.[20]

---

[20] The structure of the report is divided into: (1) scientific background and existing reference on the object of study, (2) information sources and methods used for analysis (3) clinical, economic and organizational data, (4) assessment and discussion. The types of reports can be ascribed to the following: (a) pre-assessment: based on limited reviews of bibliography, (b) emerging technology list, i.e. studies that aim to provide assessments of specific technologies; (c) full report, the most complete because they contain assessments of clinical effectiveness, cost-effectiveness and impact on technologies on the basis of clinical-epidemiological, economic, social and ethical analysis.

Once these technologies have been identified, the HTA programme becomes the mediator between NICE and working groups in charge of producing the HTA reports. In the preparing the assessments, NICE considers the aspects of both clinical effectiveness and cost-effectiveness of the technologies analyzed. These assessments allow NICE to estimate the potential savings in terms of health care spending obtainable by the NHS, if it decides to adopt a particular technology.

The producing companies (*sponsoring companies*), Scientific Societies and patient associations are always invited to submit data and information useful for the making reports, which are drawn up by a committee of experts on the basis of the information gathered and independent work carried out by HTA, commissioned to research centers chosen through a public call for tender.

In Italy, HTA has a relatively recent legislative history since it achieved legislative recognition on the evaluation of the health care "technologies" only in 2006, with PSN (Programma Sanitaria Nazionale).

Specifically, NSP 2006–2008 identified a priority necessary to develop the promotion of HTA in systemic evaluation of the technologies, "by sharing knowledge on the subject, already operating in some regional and business areas" for these reasons it is expected that "the development of the evaluation activities coordination function, known as the clearing house, is carried out by the central National Health Service technical authorities, such as the national Agency for regional Services and the National Institute of Health (ISS)".

Subsequently, in 2007 the Ministry of Health was given the legal authority to create appropriate tools for specific medical devices also through comparison of the costs compared to alternatives.

Finally, a unified conference of the State, Regions and Provinces has decided, among the strategic objectives of the Agency, "to sustain the regions in the promotion of stable regional and local planning and evaluation, the introduction and management of technological innovation and diffusion, at regional level, of the studies and assessments carried out at central level so favouring the adoption of a conduct which is consistent with results."

To this regard, the Agency has taken on the function of technical and scientific support for the promotion of regional and local HTA activities, undertaking several research projects in collaboration with the Regional Office, structures of the NHS and other institutions. A cooperation agreement between the Ministry of Health and *Agenas* has foreseen, through the same agency, to provide HTA documentation: such collaboration has allowed the contextualization, of the *Technology Assessmen*[21] proceedings with on field experimentation.

---

[21] HTA in Italy acquires a form and institutional significance following the development of a movement of interest born around cultural research projects, including the one that has led to the establishment of the Italian Network for Health Technology Assessment.

In our country, the Regions that have taken initiatives in the field of scientific HTA are Trentino, author of the "Carta del Trento", Emilia Romagna, Tuscany, Lombardy and Campania. The innovative contribution that has characterized the Region of Campania has been significant as researchers in the field have not only favoured HTA product evaluation (through, a post technology evaluation), but it has even been thought to implement *Horizon Scanning*[22] assessments. With HS there is a tendency to recognize and identify health care technologies in development, not yet on the market: their assessment is often made on the basis of projections or predictions of their possible impact on the health care system, both in clinical and management terms.

In May 2009 the first SIHHS was set up in Campania (Italian Society of *Health Horizon Scanning*) from the strong will of a group of HTA enthusiasts, teachers and doctors, all sharing the desire to seek a means with which to overcome the difficult situation characterizing the health care reality. Specifically, the SIHHS objective is to seek, through a transnational approach, innovative technologies that help firstly, to improve the quality of health care service and secondly, tend to maximize efficiency, in line with the principle of equitable distribution of recourses. The SIHHS cultural project involves the collaboration not only of public health academic institutions, but there is also a massive entrepreneurship participation in the sector of health care technologies. To date, the initiatives undertaken have been various, among these the preparation of two reports having as their objectives, one, to offer anti-pneumococcal vaccination destined to the pediatric population of the Region of Campania and the other, a low-protein diet for kidney disease. In the last chapter, the two reports prepared by SIHHS will be analyzed, in detail.

3.3 HTA and Technological Appropriateness

The need to define a function of strategic management[23] of technological resources does not only have the purpose of optimizing resources in health care, but first and foremost to guarantee[24] quality and appropriateness of the health care services

---

[22] Therefore HS, takes into account technologies at embryonic stage, and sometimes it is mere speculation, speculation, however, necessary because it is able to consider the limits and potential of a technology, even before its introduction. HS in respect to HTA has a pre strategic function assessment therefore the decision makers can and should address the resources available only to the most appropriate innovations.

[23] The term "strategy" means: "a design that emerges in a stream of decisions that position the organization with respect to the environment and from which follows the actual behavior of the organization. In addition, a strategy is a plan aimed at providing managers with guidance for future decisions" (Casati 2000).

[24] Over the years, the definition of the term "quality" has been subject to constant changes. First, Donadebian, identified the quality as the ability to better manage the balance between the benefits and risks to health, both at individual and community level (Donadebian 1988). The role of quality is marked as meeting the health care needs and at the same time to the attention of resource bonds.

provided. *Appropriateness* is a neologism that carries a central meaning of health care policy and a mandatory feature of health care services (Falcinetti 2004). The use of, appropriate, scientifically valid and socially acceptable technology accessible to all, was designated by the World Health Organization (WHO), at the International Conference in Alma Ata in 1978, with the principles of *Health for Hall*: lists of essential drugs to maximize the effectiveness and minimize costs.

The concept of appropriateness is nevertheless, stated later on, with the health care reforms of the past two decades, that were inspired, at global level, by the doctrine of public service organization in the new public management or planned market.

In this scenario, appropriateness is emerging as a characteristic of health care interventions that integrates effectiveness, efficiency[25] and economy (Falcitetti 2004). However, the first two principles are not logically separable: according to Cochrane (1972), the father of medicine based on evidence of efficacy (Evidence Based Medicine), efficiency cannot be achieved in the absence of effectiveness.

Appropriateness, in short, is to be understood as a component of health care quality, which refers to both the techno-scientific validity and acceptability and to health care benefits relevance.[26] It, also in accordance with the environmental, institutional and social reference guidelines, must be achieved by balancing the issues of consumer efficiency and effectiveness concerning the health care services.

It also becomes useful, in an operational point of view, to distinguish two different areas of application:

Clinical Appropriateness regards indication and execution of a health care intervention in such conditions that the probability of benefit outweighs the potential risk.

Organizational Appropriateness: instead, refers to, the level of assistance which must be adapted to clinically appropriate health care intervention, in terms of safety and economy of resources.

In the early 80s, in the United States of America, in response to the rising costs of public assistance programmes (*Medicare*, *Medicaid*) and face to face with the risk of potentially distortive effects of the market, assessment tools known as *utilization review* were developed. Thus, the organizational appropriateness becomes a central aspect of the health care services evaluation provided in the context of managed care, absorbing the principles of economy in the consumption of resources and operational efficiency.

The health care industry provides a person with public services to improve the quality of life (Borgonovi 2000), characterizing its system with a *labor intensive*

---

[25] There are two different types of efficiency: *allocative efficiency* evaluates various alternative interventions to decide how to distribute resources among various interventions in order to obtain the maximum benefit. *Technical efficiency* instead evaluates, the best way to achieve a certain goal.

[26] EBM is increasingly used as a scientific approach to plan health policy strategies according to the approach known as evidence-based health care representing a cardinal factor in the search for appropriate levels of healthcare policies.

nature in carrying out its activities in a "professional organizational" way through concrete health care technology, *enabling resource*.

It is no coincidence, therefore, that the attention given to the quality and appropriateness of clinical practice promoted by movements for evidence-based medicine (Evidence Based Medicine,[27] EBM) has had the merit of providing, *decision makers*, operators and health care service consumers, with "traps" of clinical efficacy evaluation, understood as a demonstrated ability of positive impact on the health and welfare of the NHS technology population.

The prospect of EBM is a crucial point that impacts directly on HTA: evidence-based medicine is the conscientious, explicit and judicious use of the best available evidence to decide which technologies to introduce. In other words, EBM is a process of self-learning in which individual patient care stimulates medical research for clinically relevant information in specialist studies.

Basically, EBM originates from two assumptions (Wallace 1997):

1. no doctor, howsoever experienced and competent, can know all the advances in clinical research;
2. many health care interventions, both diagnostic and therapeutic, have been introduced into clinical practice before being subjected to numerous clinical trials to define their efficacy that is often dubious or non-existent.

And precisely for these assumptions, the starting point in analyzing health care technology diffusion, is proven clinical efficacy, as *without which it could not be* can trigger the process of diffusion, and it is the main determinant of success/ failure.

This might seem like a trivial reflection that calls to question both innovative health care technology, which is relatively new, and the one in use. As part of the current processes of health care technology diffusion, the phases that precede "innovation", and the same phase of evaluation, not always fully address the issues of clinical efficacy. Historic studies, such as the one promoted by the *Office for Technology Assessment* (OTA 1976), or the work of McKinley (1981), have highlighted how, in the early stages of diffusion, attention is focused rather on other aspects: the evaluation of profit potential, from the producer point of view, or the system of "values" on which health care technology impacts, from a public system point of view.

On the contrary, in terms of technology therapeutic value testing, it is in this phase that error risks are structurally higher, a difficult phase in which the performance of the *randomized controller trial* is promoted to evaluate innovative technology plagued with factors such as low number of patients on which to test,

---

[27] Evidence Based Medicine (EBM) is a cultural movement that has spread rapidly in the scientific world, based on a new approach to healthcare where *"clinical decisions resulting from the integration of the experience of the physician and the use of best available scientific evidence, relative to diagnostic test accuracy, the power of prognostic factors, efficacy/safety of preventive, and rehabilitation treatment"* (Sackett 1996).

the will to place new technology on the market, trust in progress, the *desperate reaction* of adopting doctors.

The collection of evidence becomes, therefore, an essential moment in the evaluation of technology and, for this reason, one can speak of a rating system based on scientific evidence (*Evidence Based Decision Support*): the logical consequence, appears to be the development of a decision-making system based on the above mentioned assumptions.[28]

3.4 HTA and Decision-Making Processes

Among the variables that characterize a HTA process, one that more than others appears to have a predominant role, is the organizational variable that is also considered as a barrier in the adoption and diffusion of new technology in the event that the latter is not "*professional friendly*".[29] The underlying cause is given by the fear that innovation can affect the balance of power within organizations or affect existing practices and procedures.

Positive professional attitudes towards new technology depends, above all, on the system of values and experience: for this reason, training is an important tool to support the adoption and development of the context, since it directly affects professional skills, skills however, may not be enough. When formation is primarily training for the use of new technology, its success is influenced by the position of the personal "learning curve", in turn a function of past experience, motivation manifested and producer assistance.

In short, experts struggle to gain and maintain their professional autonomy as "control of their technology by a group of operators is what distinguishes a professional group from other types of associations": the adoption of new technology can make a difference in the evolution of professional sub-groups that specialize in taking advantage of the breaking points of the learning curves of the main professional group. The ultra specialization induced by technological innovation (Green 1988) is the leading professional competitive strategy: it creates a circular relationship of mutual effect between the development of new specialties brought about by new technologies and the *technologiztion* induced by the rise of new specialties.

---

[28] Methods to generate new data on the effects of a new medical technology are: Randomized controller trials (RCT), Short study, Case control study. The interpretation of the tests involves the classification of the studies, conferring to each of them importance and the possibility to include them or not in the summary. There are two methods of synthesizing information: the non-quantitative review of the bibliography (such revisions consist in summaries of existing reference selected and appropriately assessed) and the *meta-analysis* (refers to a group of statistical techniques that combine data of multiple studies in order to achieve results and quantitative estimates).

[29] Organizational barriers are, in general, the lack of motivation of doctors in action, lack of managerial support and factors related to the productive ability of the organization.

One of the difficulties present in situations of more acute collaboration is the definition of problems and to find the most appropriate solutions for achieving long-term goals.

Many people experience difficulty not only in defining a problem with someone else, a discomfort which is accepted within a group,[30] but also in accepting and making the solutions produced together their own.

The discomfort related to sharing is even more evident when the decision to be accepted is made by others, and occurs regardless of the quality of the solution, confirming the fact that it arises from "how" and "who" and not "from what" was decided.

These situations are very common in health care, because of the different cultures involved characterized by considerable autonomy that affects every collaborative situation.

The difficulty in accepting decisions is therefore not related to the quality of the decisions, but the fact that a person feels that his space of autonomy is threatened, if he accept the solutions proposed by others.

Even in situations of collaboration with a strong technical content, it may happen that people, feeling that their autonomy is threatened, object to a decision by implementing issues of principle.

Other examples of problems of integration between different cultures are found when examining the collaboration between technicians and managers in health care organizations,[31] when, for fear of losing autonomy, some requests from the other party are practically not implemented.

All this is connected to a decision-making process and confirms the practical importance of that particular skill namely, *decision making and problem solving*.

In general, decision-making should, lead to a very specific goal, not surprisingly, the verb "to decide" contains the Latin root *caedere* (to cut) and expresses the concept of the end of a process, it is quite clear that the more situations are complex, the more the fact of bringing, some processes and the quality of the conclusion which is reached, to an end, they are elements of great importance for the development of organizational action.

Decisions must be understood as rational, simultaneous and optimizing processes based on a perfect knowledge of reality[32]: in reference to the decision-making process, Simon (1947) points out how the acting parties make choices

---

[30] Today we are witnessing a logical and practical reorganization of health care organizations based on integrated work, not always accompanied by an accurate assessment of the skills that this change can bring, and are still considered a natural gift or a "mechanical" process resulting from different ways of working.

[31] The collaboration between engineers and managers within a HTA program, is of fundamental importance if we consider HTA as a bridge between science and politics.

[32] To form complex skills and competencies we must make use of many tools and it is necessary to think about training opportunities in which to provide practical experience on which to reflect, because for the development of skills it is definitely more beneficial to reflect on real-life experiences rather than simulated ones, i.e. not representative of the daily life of the person.

under conditions of restricted rationality, following a sequential/iterative and satisfying process, based on, in a more or less conscious way, models, seen as selective and simplified representations of reality.

Decision-making processes act as operational mechanisms[33] and are characterized by information input from a system of choices and an output of actions and information; thus, the role of the information system that constitutes the essential elements of the entire decision-making process appears evident.

The decision represents the findings of a complex process through which, with appropriate information support; there is an evaluation of the multiple alternatives within the options that tend to achieve the objectives more effectively.[34]

The decision-making system is divided into three sub-systems: strategic decisions, tactical decisions, and operational decisions. The first invests fundamental aspects of health care companies and makes its influence felt over a substantial period originating from difficult operations which are irreversible if the term is short. The latter propose themselves as instruments for implementing strategic decisions, while the third is characterized by limited discretion: they are therefore structured and originate operating data mostly reversible.[35]

It is clear that we must also define the space within which to develop decision-making processes and this means identifying which variables determine it: it refers specifically to the institutional variables, company variables and individual variables.

The decision-making autonomy is, in fact, strongly influenced by national and regional legislation, the targets and the national and local programmes (institutional variables). To these aspects we need to add the limits arising from joint organization that defines the responsibilities and procedures for carrying out the processes of production and that gives the authority understood as an exercise of normative powers and access to information (business variables).

The institutional and company variables end up identifying decision making space therefore of an action defined in a neutral and objective way, but it is

---

[33] The operating mechanisms are one of the main dimensions of company organizational analysis. The term "operational mechanism", refers to the processes that govern the functioning of an organization, inducing appropriate stimuli to individuals and groups within a business organization. While the organizational structure defines the basic elements of the system of organizational roles and responsibilities, operational mechanisms represent the dynamic operation of the organizational system and cover an articulated variety of items. The operating mechanisms concern the following processes within the organization: communication processes, decision-making processes, the processes of planning and monitoring and evaluation processes.

[34] The importance of goal setting in decision-making is widely emphasized by Simon (1947) who correctly points out that the existence of a unique opportunity to assess the accuracy of the decision: refers to the purpose.

[35] Simon then divides the decisions in planned and unplanned. Decisions are programmed to the extent that they are made known and repetitive and a specific procedure was destined for their allocation. The decisions are not programmed to the extent that they are new, unstructured and occasional.

necessary to point out that every decision-making process refers to the ability of the operators and their motivations (individual variables).

The level of HTA process is directly proportional to the dimensions of decision-making space, in the sense that the effect of the evaluation process on the decision-making function is greater if the decision making space available is large. It has been affirmed that HTA is intended to provide information constituting a bridge between knowledge and decisional levels: the information useful for all decision-making processes is produced through HTA.

Starting from this consideration, Baptist states that: "the ultimate goal and the main reason for technology evaluation is to promote the transfer of the technical and scientific approach into decision making, creating continuous links between research, data, objectives and decisions."

It is on the bases of these assumptions that a process of *"Technology Assessment"* is organized within a global decision-making process, therefore, considering how a method of processing information sustains future decisions.

A HTA process consists of several steps, linked to each other.

The first phase of the process of *technology assessment* is characterized by the identification and explanation of clinical needs: there are attempts to determine whether a given solution may or may not be "appropriate". The term *"problem solving"*, in this particular definition is not used, as its data technology that does not always derive from the need to solve a problem. In fact, the potential benefits arising from the introduction of new technologies, could themselves, represent a need.

In the context of this clinical need, the potential to improve the benefits must be represented by three factors: (a) potential relative to the improvement of health care *outcomes*,[36] (b) potential for reducing costs, (c) potential relative, to the simplification of the health care services supply processes.

The next *step* is clinical applicability that is; a macro-analysis designed to identify potential technological solutions, compare them and identify, the optimal technology area, if there is one. The main task of the *step* is to transfer the clinical

---

[36] "Outcomes" is intended as:

(a) any possible outcome that may result from a specific intervention in a given situation;
(b) one of the possible consequences of assistance in a general problem of medical care;
(c) the actual result of an activity and one of the most important parameters in the evaluation of effectiveness;
(d) only what is connected to the conditions of patient or population well-being, for the quality and quantity of life of social and health care intervention addressees.

"Output" is intended as:

(a) the health care service as a result of a process;
(b) summery of the results of an intervention aimed at modifying the spontaneous functioning of a system;
(c) amount of the benefits or effects obtained by the use of certain means.

(*Glossary of quality and organization*, Monographs no. 1/2000, Regione Lazio).

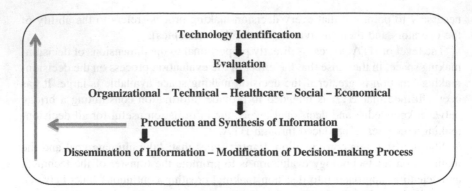

Technology Identification
↓
Evaluation
↓
Organizational – Technical – Healthcare – Social – Economical
↓
Production and Synthesis of Information
↓
Dissemination of Information – Modification of Decision-making Process

Fig. 3.1 Bureaucratic process of HTA. *Source* author processing

needs into operating parameters suitable when comparing the positive and negative impact of new alternative technologies in realistic operational conditions.

Step 3 is concerned with the evaluation of the alternatives in the technology field identified in the clinical applicability analysis. This phase of the *assessment* process is a very empirical phase: it requires accurate assessment of the existing alternatives on the market, assessment to be carried out under standard operating conditions. The fourth phase consists of its approval by the authority, but it is also the phase in which most of the initiatives are blocked due to the difficulties that arise at this point.

The team (multi-professional and multi-disciplinary) that deals with *technology assessment* needs to develop an appropriate implementation plan for the purpose of introducing the technology. Lastly there is a *follow-up* phase.

Following this process, HTA performs a function of "organizer" as it identifies the lines of action to achieve goals as effectively as possible. There are basically three aspects that characterize HTA:

- Identification of the different alternatives possible;
- Evaluation of the pros and cons of the alternatives considered;
- Evaluation and comparison of expected results and objectives (Fig. 3.1).

3.4.1 The Implementation of a HTA Process

The gradual decentralization of activities today, even at single service supply company level, allows us to provide three main levels of development and dissemination of HTA process (Fig. 3.2):

- **Macro,** or the level of health care policies for which HTA, according to a now well-established approach, supports *policy making* and the research for

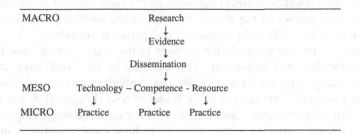

MACRO Research
↓
Evidence
↓
Dissemination
↓
MESO Technology – Competence - Resource
↓   ↓   ↓
MICRO Practice Practice Practice

Fig. 3.2 HTA and decision-making levels. *Source* adapted by Cicchetti (2004)

appropriateness of clinical practice, serving as a bridge that connects science and research to centralized *decision making*;

- **Meso,** or the level represented by individual companies that provide welfare services. The role of HTA is to support managerial decision making in search of efficiency and effectiveness when providing health care services, to reduce the high variability of clinical practice and organizational innovation at processes, technology and infrastructure level;
- **Micro** or the level of clinical practice, i.e. the interaction between experts and patients, which is also influenced by the specific organizational characteristics, operational powers and a unique set of individual skills and knowledge.

The rationality and success of the diffusion process of health care technologies within the real health care systems depends on, at first approximation, the equilibrium of the variables, that try to adapt the essential dimensions of health care technology assessment in the health care *Technology Assessment* sample model, already proposed by Banta (1993), to the characteristics of the decentralized health care system set up in Italy at the end of the NHS reform process.

Therefore, it may be concluded, that the success of the diffusion of innovative health care technology is a combined effect of three factors and the influence of the role of the acting parties who control them.

It is, above all the demonstrated clinical efficacy of the technology introduced (the role of the patient), in the sense that innovation must be able to improve the health conditions of the patient and, in more general terms, produce a positive impact on the welfare of the community. Furthermore, there must be compatibility and utility between the institutional objectives[37] and the limit of resources (role of the company decision-maker). Practically, the adoption of health care technology must be perceived as useful for the achievement of institutional objectives and compatible with the limit of resource, increasing the space of action available to the company to cope with the demand for health care.

---

[37] The importance of referring to the company institutional framework as a higher-level element of the structure of a company is underlined (Airoldi et al. 1994).

Finally, there must be professional autonomy[38]: technological innovation must have a positive impact on the *modus operandi* of the medical profession and be consistent with the skills and professional and personal incentive.

The role of the company decision-maker is the source which now features greater variability and dynamism. The changes in the NHS have certainly expanded strategic space left for the health care authorities and the activities of the "Regione Campania", considered as the leader of SSR (Longo 2005; Scaletti and Belfiore 2010). In this space, decisions in health care technology adoption are a moment of highly strategic significance, as technological resource is in fact a competitive guiding variable in business strategies.

However, at decentralized level, the lack of management skills and limited resources to invest can distort choice rationality favouring a focus on short-term effects to the detriment of a broader evaluation, giving rise to the phenomena of strategic myopia that needs to be considered (Borgonovi 2000).

With regards to professional variables, there is the need to engage and establish an atmosphere of collaboration among experts (clinicians, economists, engineers, biomedical scientists, ethicists) establishing the real organizational relationships.[39]

Although this phenomenon appears to be widely known and debated, it is appropriate and necessary to point out that in the health care sector, unlike in other service sectors, innovation cannot be produced without the explicit acceptance of the operators and health care technology experts who will be using it.

Allocation of resources and prioritization is developed through a process of continuous negotiation and mutual adjustment between the rationality of corporate decisions and the rationality of experts, as the adoption of a new technology has a direct impact on the medical profession (in terms *modus operandi*, training needs, culture, values and social status of doctors) and cannot under any circumstances be a decision imposed from above.

In such a scenario, the organizational variable refers mostly to the personal role of the acting parties involved in decision-making, especially the professionals who reaffirm their own layout of how to respond to care needs.

To reach a heuristic representation of the variables that have different ways of disseminating technology within business systems, it is therefore necessary to provide at least one classification of the variables involved in the process of health technology dissemination, considering the institutional variables, the business

---

[38] Clinical autonomy involves a system of accountability where, in the light of rigid constraints in allocating resources, significant spaces of autonomy in the ways resources are used, is created (Zangrandi 1998).

[39] In the health sector, organizational relationships differ from relationships in healthcare. In fact, the first identify all activities not directly aimed at the patient/client of the healthcare company, while the latter refer to all those activities strictly clinical that relate to the content of the work related to it (i.e. hospitalization, the protocol to follow, etc.). This distinction is important in understanding the responsibilities (Zangrandi 1998). Earlier, it is also identified the presence of clinical autonomy as the fundamental characteristic able to guarantee the patient-physician relationship in the NHS organization.

variables and individual variables (determining role of the organizational variable).

3.5 Multi-Disciplinary Aspects of a HTA Process

When we speak of experts and decision-makers, we have to take clearly into account the changes brought about by the various legislative measures following one another over the years[40] that to date, have brought the top management to make strategic and operational choices to deal with, in the best possible way, the constraints of the contingent environment respecting the rules and subjects in the interest of the operating company.

The HTA process is characterized by the different points of view that need to be taken into account at the moment of new "*technology*" introduction: we must take into account the plurality of decision-making centres, the fragmentation of competencies[41] and functional interdependencies that arise.

The heterogeneity of the activities that characterize a HTA process (they range from the economic sphere, to the clinical, ethical, juridical one) inevitably implies the presence of very in-depth and specialized technical skills. To explain the strategic choices, individual and collective behaviour and the results that determine the HTA process, "organizational competence" must be considered, which is intended as the way of using resource and knowledge in the organizational processes in order to reach the desired outcomes. Individual knowledge and organizational skills are combined for the implementation of a process (in our case a HTA process), contributing to the production and evaluation of "health care technology".[42]

In fact, various studies have shown that the adoption of "new technology" produces a profound redefinition of workplace relationships in the organizational

---

[40] In this regard Lega (2003a, b) stresses the need to redefine the micro-organizational structure of Italian hospitals aimed at identifying roles and responsibilities in managing the activities that ensure better development and control of innovative dynamics order to: (a) build a work environment conducive to innovation and to steer the selection of investments (strategic profile), (b) Identify and strengthen the company roles and responsibilities to safeguard innovation and entrepreneurship, (c) strengthen the operational mechanisms for the governed management of the innovation process (management profile).

[41] The term competence is generally used extensively, particularly in the last decade, with the introduction of the "competency model" so eclectic, to propose approaches that are very different from each other and that are often ignored.

[42] In planning the combination modality of individual and organizational skills, management is "bound" by institutional factors that tend to limit the number of viable options and choices. However, at the same time, managerial choices of combination and recombination of skills and knowledge are grafted into a dynamic organization that independently induces a continuous and routine recombination, of skill and knowledge.

system, inducing a potential evolution in the repertoire of general organizational routines.

Health care technology, in other words, is a mediator of the interaction modalities within health care organizations: the effect of technology adoption is not what is understood by incidental tradition,[43] that is to say that it does not give the management suggestions of most suitable organizational solutions in the light of options pre-established through a process of rational nature. The introduction of a new technology induces specific professional interrelations of the different skills that are progressively refined and crystallized during work routine: skills are modified regardless of the formal structure thus, constituting a real "community of practice".[44]

With the adoption of new health care technology, professionals will tend to recreate those forms of mutual interdependence that, in accordance with professional autonomy, ensure the resolution of problems of employment. In a HTA process, alongside the rational assessments or better economic, one must take into account the combinations of skill modality that is, however, influenced by indications coming from the institutional logics.[45]

The methods and operational tools for the process of technology assessment are increasingly shared and harmonized at European level. The opportunity of a harmonization, even at National level, seems auspicable by many interested parties, not only the operators and evaluators, but also the industry and patients.[46]

In Italy, the process of institutionalization analysis is accompanied by the evaluation of the two factors "enabling" the correct implementation of a HTA process:

1. The availability of specific professional skills in the application of complex methods;
2. A sharing of methods and procedures among interested parties.

---

[43] In the contingent approach the generic and broad notion of "environment" has been traced back to "types" an ideal in respect to which the various contributions have correlated consistent structural situations. Lawrence and Lorsh (1967) by certain and uncertain environment.

[44] This is particularly true in hospitals where the nature of work imposes those patterns of cooperation difficult to capture in standard formal procedures (Cicchetti and Lomi 2001).

[45] Institutional logic means "the set of cultural—cognitive beliefs, of the regulatory framework and regulatory systems that ensure a sector stability and significance" (Scott and Meyer 1983). This definition reflects a meaning of the term "institutional" typical of the neo-institutionalism theory (Selznick 1957; Powell and DiMaggio 1991; Scott and Meyer 1983), is enlarged compared to the one commonly adopted within the healthcare sector which refers to the very intensive regulatory aspects.

[46] Therefore, company management, finds itself managing multiple relationships with the various stakeholders. Of particular importance are, individual citizens, who ask for, directly or indirectly, efficiency and effectiveness, central and regional institutions that ask for appropriate behaviour and respect of economic and planning restrictions, in defining the allocation of resources.

Skills are essential in the management of a process that finds its fundamental characteristics in the sturdiness of its methods and transparency. The development of methodological, epidemiological and pharma-economic skills appears fundamental to support this evolution.

The sharing of methods and approaches among industry, *policy makers*, researchers and patients is essential to achieve an effective and sustainable HTA model.

References

Airoldi G, Brunetti G, Coda V (1994) Economia Aziendale. Il Mulino, Bologna

Banta HD, Luce BR (1993) Tecnologia sanitaria e la sua valutazione: una prospettiva internazionale. Oxford University Press, New York

Battista RN (2006) Expanding the scientific basis of health technology assessment: a research agenda for the next decade. Int J Technol Assess Healthc 22:275–282

Borgonovi E (1996, 2000, 2002) Principi e sistemi aziendali per le amministrazioni pubbliche. Egea, Milano

Casati G (2000) Programmazione e controllo di gestione nelle aziende sanitarie. McGraw-Hill, New York

Cicchetti A (2004) La progettazione organizzativa. Franco Angeli, Milano

Cicchetti A, Lomi A (2001) Aspetti relazionali ed attributivi della va-riabilità nelle performance delle unità organizzative sanitarie. In: Co-sta G (ed) Flessibilità e performance, Atti Convegno di Padova 2001

Coates JF, Jarrat J (1992) Course workbook: technology assessment. Anticipating the consequences of technology choices. The George Washington University Press, Washington, 17 Aug 1992

Cochrane A (1972) Publication by the Nuffield provincial hospitals trust of his book effectiveness and efficiency—random reflections on health services WHO

Donadebian A (1988) La qualità dell'assistenza sanitaria: principi e metodologie di valutazione, ed. La nuova Italia scientifica, Firenze

Falcinetti N (2004) Rapporto sanità 2004. L'appropriatezza in sanità: uno strumento per migliorare la pratica clinica. Il Mulino, Bologna

Goodman CS (1998) Hta 101: introduction to health technology assessment. National Library of Medicine, Bethesda

Green A (1988) The state of the art versus the state of the science: the diffusion of the new medical technologies into practice. Int J Technol Asses 4:5–26

Kisseck W (1994) Medicines dilemmas: infinite needs versus finite resource. Yale University Press, New Haven and London

Lamberti C (1998) Le apparecchiature biomediche e la loro gestione. Patron editore, Bologna

Laurence PR, Lorsch JW (1967) Organization and environment: managing differentation and integration. Graduate School of Business Administartion, Harvard University Press, Boston

Lega F (2003a) Il marketing in sanità: una questione di prospettive. Sa-nità pubblica e privata 4:448–457

Lega F (2003b) Orientare all'innovazione dell'ospedale. Aspetti strate-gici, organizzativi e gestionali. Mecosan 47:23–38

Longo F (2005) Governance dei network di pubblico interesse. Egea, Milano

McKinley JB (1981) From promising report to standard procedure: seven stages in the career of a medical innovation. Health Soc 59:374–409

Office of Technology Assessment (OTA) (1976) Development of medical technology. Opportunities for assessment. US Government Printing Office, Washington

Powell WW, Di Maggio PJ (1991) The new istituzionalism in organizational analisys. The University of Chicago Press, Chicago

Sakett DL (1996) Evidence based medicine: what is and what isn't. BMJ 312:1–72

Scaletti A, Belfiore P (2010) Il ruolo delle tecnologie e dell'Health technology assessment (HTA) in un sistema sanitario. Nium rivista on line

Scott WR, Meyer JW (1983) Organizational environments: ritual and rationality. Sage, Beverly Hill

Selzenik P (1957) Leadership in administration. Harper-Row, New York

Simon HA (1947) Administrative behaviour. The Free Press, New York

Wallace EZ (1997) Doing the right thing right: is evidence based medicine the answer. Ann Intern Med 127:91–94

Zangrandi A (1998) Amministrazione delle aziende sanitarie pubbli-che. Giuffrè, Milano